BRIGHT LIGHT IN THE SKY

SURENDRA KUMAR SAGAR

DISCLAIMER   (SECOND EDITION)

The author and the publisher hereby declare that the title and the contents of the book are not meant to evoke or hurt any religious or communal sentiments. The author and the publishing house have undertaken all reasonable and prudent efforts to ensure that the sentiments of any person, country, legal system, religion or community are not deliberately hurt.

COPYRIGHT (SECOND EDITION)

means, including photocopying, recording or other electronic or mechanical methods, without the prior written permission of the author, except in the case of brief quotations embodied in critical reviews and certain other noncommercial uses permitted by copyright law. For permission requests, write to the author at the email address below.

sks@total-environment.com

DEDICATION

This book is dedicated to our loved ones who have departed. They all come back. Consciousness is not just our Birth right, it is also our Death right.

PRAISE FOR SURENDRA KUMAR SAGAR AND HIS BOOKS

BRIGHT LIGHT IN THE SKY

"Surendra Kumar Sagar's third book, 'Bright Light In The Sky' follows the trajectory of his earlier books in being profound, provocative and probing. Reading Mr. Sagar's latest contribution, I am reminded of Edward Gibbon's 'Decline and Fall of the Roman Empire,' which is a narrative through a thousand years. We see the greatness of that Empire at its height, its military organisation, its provincial administration, its welter of races, the rise and clash of two religions, and the passage of Greek philosophy into Christian theology. But it is Gibbon who speaks throughout this 'history'. Mr. Sagar's saga resonates with similar vibrations. The ideas, events and instances described in his book are not his creation, but the voice you hear is the inimitable one of Surendra Kumar Sagar, weaving a tapestry of thought and philosophy, ushering a grand confluence of ideas and conundrums, displaying the need for convergence of imagination, as a compass for our elusive quest for a sense of the future, on the journey yet to be."

Shoumen Palit Austin Datta
Director MIT
Academician, Author, Research Scientist at MIT.

"I am very happy to learn about your new book. It is a very interesting one. I wish you continued success in achieving a nuclear peril free world."

Prof. M.S. Swaminathan
Founder Chairman and Chief Mentor UNESCO Chair in Eco Technology
M.S. Swaminathan Research Foundation.

"This book is a more elaborate and updated version of his earlier two books with a similar background on the subject. Sagar is more focused on the nuclear landscape and has not given adequate stress on the likelihood of a chemical/germ-warfare or climate change and environmental pollution overtaking/combining with nuclear antagonisms between nations to increase the risk and hasten the end of humanity. While a nuclear Armageddon may bring about the end instantaneously, these other factors may bring about the end far more lingeringly over a period of decades and/or years, if nothing is done effectively to arrest the trend of movements with respect to these factors or prevent such an Armageddon from happening. It is the world's misfortune that the US along with a few developed nations is in the forefront of opposition to climate change.

I wish the book resounding success and as per schedule at turning nuclear, ecological and other hawks into doves soon enough for the continued survival and evolution of life on earth."

A.K.Chandrashekhar
Retired Finance Executive with interest in Science, Philosophy and Social Well Being.

Mr. Sagar`s "third book is a true reflection of his own erudite and eclectic self. Since he is a structural engineer himself, his book presents a cornucopia of fabulously structured thoughts and concepts. Taking a leap of faith, one can bring in several similes and similarities with our own ancient scriptures. The triumvirate of Body, Mind and Soul is presented in the form of Reality, Information and the Right Value System - Good Sense. The psychosomatic interactions are paralleled with the mutual influence of Reality and Information, along with the serpentine DNA like shape of such influences. And then Mr. Sagar presents the ultimate conundrum - the very survival of Homo Sapiens a la Yuval Harari. Through a willowy wizardry of equations, it is predicted that if we humans can manage to survive any nuclear holocaust for the next ten millennia, then we are pretty much assured of a perpetual existence.

In his book Mr. Sagar plumbs the depths of unfathomable profundity and covers an extraordinary canvas of eternal expanses of Time and Space. Weaving through these unthinkable discontinuities is his very unique concept of the Travelling Cosmic Mind - which is like the unifying force envisaged by quantum physicists and atomic scientists. It would be extremely interesting to look forward to Mr. Sagar's fourth book after Six Words, Intelligent Field and this Bright Light In The Sky, to wallow once again in a continuum which is both intuitive and counter-intuitive simultaneously!!"

Prof. Shashi K Sharma
Visiting Faculty, Trainer and Advisor for ETHICS and CSR; BE (Mech) from MBM Engg. College, Jodhpur, MBA from IIM, Ahmedabad and M.S. from MIT, USA.

``This is the third book of Surendra Kumar Sagar, a trilogy on Nuclear proliferation, possible nuclear war scenarios, International geo-politic and power games, and where the world stands now, all set into a philosophic and scientific background. Mr. Sagar is a structural engineer yet displays a remarkable understanding of the heart of quantum world, its implications and possible connections with the human mind and consciousness, all via the `Information in the field``

Dr ASHOK KUMAR JAIN .. Ex Head of the Physics Department I.I.T.Roorkee. .. National Award winning Nuclear Scientist

``Bright Light In The Sky is a non-fiction work that has the pace of a Michael Crichton novel in its tonality! A rare feat by the author Surendra Kumar Sagar! He has brought philosophy, and nuclear-geo-politics in a tone of ordinary conversations beautifully! I could not find a single word in the book from start to finish inauthentic in any way. An excellent piece of writing, reminding me of the writings of the Nobel Prize winning Mathematician and author BERTRAND RUSSELL. A masterly putting together of science, astronomy, philosophy and geo-politics! A rare authentic voice! What Sagar has done is taken the complexity of theories of someone like Immanuel Kant's CRITIQUE of PURE REASON and put it in the language of Bertrand Russell!!!

Congratulations on the brilliant work!``

DEEPAK SINHA .. RASA AUR DRAMA TIMES .. PUNE

``Bright Light in the Sky is an eye-opener to the Nuclear Geopolitical landscape of the world. In this analytical and deep thought out work, the author Surendra Kumar Sagar presents a counter philosophy that presents solutions to some very toxic political and religious issues.

A must-read, this book includes the Hiroshima bombing and the 9/11 attack and relevance of various factors or "information in the field", that may have led to these events. The Pugwash Conferences and the Doomsday Clock are discussed in detail in the book and Mr. Sagar's perspective and analysis will give you a more logically explained assessment of the current global scenario where we have about 20,000 nuclear warheads located at several locations world-wide and – most of them not in safe hands.

The author is a keen observer of events in the international arena, and the nuclear stockpile appears to be his primary concern. He provides an in-depth analysis on what's going wrong in the world and offers solutions to preventing humanity from future nuclear self-destruction. In the process he becomes a participator. ``

SUDHAKAR BAL HANNDA .. (On Amazon)

SIX WORDS

"Six Words is an autobiographical epic story. Epic in the dictionary sense means 'extending beyond the usual or ordinary, especially in size or scope.'

Sagar brings his personal journey to the Big Bang origin of the universe with "I am a quark." He progresses to become an atom of hydrogen, then helium, and finally explodes out of a supernova towards earth as a carbon atom, as our planetary system has formed. On earth he becomes an organic molecule and after millions of years he finally becomes a structural engineer.

This book is a tour de force of the major physical sciences, theology and philosophy. Sagar goes deeply into each of these, explaining in clear terms very complex subjects. The book then moves to a hypothetical seminar wherein major scientists and philosophers gather to compare notes and thinking. Einstein is there along with Erwin Schrodinger, Charles Sherrington, John Wheeler, Eugene Wigner and many other top scientists of history.

This is a major five-star book written by a serious student, thinker and observer of the sciences of the universe. The book's aim is to draw religion and science together in a way that leaves established scientific laws and rules intact. Six Words do exactly that. I will leave it to the reader to have the joy of uncovering Sagar's Six Words."

Dr. Clifton K Meador
Author of the best selling 'Fascinoma'.

"A treatise that ponders the law of physics, history of the cosmos, the nature of God and the fate of mankind. It is a kind of autobiography of his existence, starting with the formation of his constituent subatomic particles. It begins with a brief, engaging account of cosmology from the Big Bang through the evolution of life. The book then turns to more involved explorations of advanced physics, including the mysteries of Heisenberg's uncertainty principle, 'quantum entanglement' and the relativistic paradoxes of travel near the speed of light.

The book's sixth chapter comprises of a fanciful 'seminar' of great thinkers - from Immanuel Kant and Albert Einstein to contemporary physicist Freeman Dyson. All this background sets up a section of Sagar's own philosophical speculations, that mix topics such as the anthropic principle stating that fundamental constants must be able to support the life forms that observe them - with the quantum mechanics mysticism.

Sagar theorises that God is an abstract 'all intelligent omnipresent infinite mind' and that humans may eventually merge into the divine 'super consciousness'. Our main task is to avoid blowing ourselves up in the next few centuries - a disaster that Sagar considers a near certainty unless everyone works for world peace."

Kirkus Reviews

———

"In Six Words, the author Surendra Kumar Sagar integrates the works of some of the greatest scientists and thinkers into a discussion in a parallel universe. He fuses quantum physics with psychology, to develop a philosophy that brings Science and Religion together."

The Hindu

———

"Words of Wisdom - Science, Philosophy and Religion come together in Surendra Kumar Sagar's fascinating debut 'Six Words.' Sagar uses quantum physics as the backdrop, against which he investigates intricate philosophical questions. Impressive in its scope, Six Words discusses some of the most pressing topics of our time, including the existence of a probabilistic universe, the notion of 'one mind' as well as the meaning of God and Religion. Sagar ultimately manages to raise the question of how humans can come together to change the course of history."

Bangalore Mirror

INTELLIGENT FIELD

"Intelligent Field, 'IF' by Mr. Sagar is in many ways a continuation of his previous work 'Six Words'. The foundation of 'IF' may be traced in 'Six Words'. Both the books present an unusual mix of western philosophy, modern physics and religion, in a background of the current world polity. Sagar is a keen observer of events in the international arena, and the nuclear stockpile seems to be his main concern, as it has the capability to annihilate humans from the face of the earth. When there is a weapon available, a situation for its use will arise eventually; this is a source of concern. Unravelling the inner secrets of a nucleus, man captured the ultimate power which is the source of all energy in the universe. This made him feel invincible. But invincible against whom? It has pitted man against man.

History of the world is full of wars. Religions have also been used and are still being used to fight wars and perpetuate conflicts which severely undermine the modern human values. I may however point out that what we call modern human values, have been deeply engrained in the great philosophies of the Eastern religions since ages. These are not new to us in India. But somewhere in the course of history, we lost them in a struggle for survival. 'IF' lays bare the underlying struggle that is still on in the world in different forms. Sagar raises important questions about the origins and the hidden nature of these perpetual games of power and survival. Are there any unknown dimensions to these questions and happenings?

Sagar is an engineer by profession, but he displays a deep understanding of the heart of modern quantum mechanics, which he has used to propound the concept of an Intelligent Field. The flow of information in this field keeps everything connected and the evolution of the universe happens in a self-consistent way. Our minds and the information therein are also part of this field and therefore affect each other. This is an interesting concept like a Cosmic Mind or 'Param Brahma' in Vedic literature. Survival of the human race critically depends on the flow of the right kind of information in the field. The 'IF' itself may not have any intentions or motives. It cannot therefore ensure our survival. It is the information that we put in the field and the way we interact that will probably decide the future course for humans. This is where the author tries to make a vehement appeal to all those in the know of things, to attempt to save our extinction. It puts the concepts of mind, consciousness and soul into focus, while compelling us to think about the motives of our existence and if there is any deeper meaning to it. Keeping rational thinking and science at the top, it tries to ponder on the ways of merging science with religions of the world. In other words, it argues - what we need is a scientific religious philosophy to save us from the impending nuclear catastrophe.

It is a highly readable book with a large number of original references and cross-references to support the ideas presented by the author. It is remarkable that the author has been able to convey his ideas in simple words even though they may appear weird at times. Mr. Sagar has persistently pursued these ideas for many decades and the book represents the essence of his thinking and possible solutions to the problems that mankind faces. It is sure to make its mark in the world.

Prof. Ashok Kumar Jain
Award winning Nuclear Physicist and Ex Head of the
Physics Dept. IIT, Roorkee.

``Intelligent Field by the immensely gifted author, Surendra Kumar Sagar, is a mind-expanding look at what he refers to as the Intelligent Field, a sort of Traveling Cosmic Mind that controls nature, but it's the `Information` in the field and the flow of such information in the field that is responsible for everything that happens in the universe , including the imparting of Intelligence to the field. As mentioned in the Foreword of the book, within this `Intelligent Field` is a universal mind, that gives us "consciousness."

Intelligent Field is a follow-up, of sorts, to Sagar's book, Six Words. Both Intelligent Field and Six Words have a cross-disciplinary approach and are deeply philosophical. In

Intelligent Field, as in Six Words, a wide variety of topics get incorporated into a heady mix, with Sagar always optimistic in the potential for the human race, but also pointing out how events unfolding in the United States and globally could lead to the possible end of human life on the planet Earth.

Sagar is not a prophet of gloom and doom in *Intelligent Field*, but he does mention that humans are getting closer and closer to midnight, as far as the Doomsday Clock goes. There is still time left to pull humanity back from the brink of potential extinction, but it can only be accomplished only if certain measures are taken before it is too late.

In part, *Intelligent Field* is a snapshot in time, presenting a picture of the state of humanity in the time before Donald Trump was elected president of the United States. Sagar writes about the potential that humans can achieve, and also the very real possibility that they might be hurtling towards self-destruction. However, Sagar writes in chapter 1B, "An Integrated Approach Toward Convergence," about how mankind can change the course it is on, through avoiding nuclear war, a convergence of religion with science, resolving conflicts between nations and within nations, and eliminating nuclear threat, altogether.

Albert Einstein and Bertrand Russell were two of the main people behind the start of the Pugwash Conferences, which, as Sagar discusses at some length, began in 1957, and were attended by scientists, scholars and public figures desiring to figure out ways to avoid armed conflicts and seek solutions for global problems. Later, nuclear scientist Joseph Rotblat was another of the important proponents of the Pugwash

Conferences, dedicating his life, as Sagar writes, "to peace and the prevention of nuclear wars."

Some of the other topics Sagar writes about in Intelligent Field is the possibility of how the travelling cosmic mind is linked with Relativity, with entropy, with quantum entanglement, and in the philosophical sense linked with Einstein's cosmic religious feeling. .There is also an in-depth discussion on Mind, Consciousness and the Soul, and on the importance of `Information` in defining reality. Sagar also revisits his previous book, *Six Words*, and includes comments and correspondence he has had with others about the book.

Intelligent Field by Surendra Kumar Sagar is a mixture of philosophy, science, religion and rational thinking, a perfect book for anyone who enjoys pondering the answers to life's "Big Questions," and what direction humanity is headed towards. It is also a Must Read for fans of Sagar's book, *Six Words*. Intelligent Field* is destined to become a classic, a book that is sure to make a valuable addition to your reading lists and personal libraries.``

DOUGLAS. R. COBB (Bestsellersworld.com)

`` <u>The rainbow with awakening on one end and enlightenment on the other...</u>

The invisible `Intelligent Field` with the ever-increasing information in the field is in control of what happens in the universe. The processing of information is a continuous process. The universe appears to be a quantum computer, that computes its own behaviour. At some stage in the remote past `Intelligence` arrived in the field, and started processing

the information in ways, designed to bring in life and
consciousness to understand itself. In the present Eon of the
Universe, the permanence of consciousness appears to be
ensured by the idea of a `traveling cosmic mind` that travels
forwards and backwards in time so as to always remain in the
Stelliferrous (liveable) era of the universe, where stars are
shining and life and consciousness is flourishing.
This book `Intelligent Field` by Surendra Kumar Sagar is a
guiding light towards `Enlightenment`. The future could be
bright for all of us. However, there is a roadblock. The current
information in the field shows the `Intelligent Field` as so
severely contaminated, and the `emblematic nuclear clock` so
close to midnight, that extinction of the human race becomes
a possibility. Professor M S Swaminathan, Father of India's
'Green Revolution,' in his Foreword considers the book as
timely and significant. It could bring about an awareness about
the necessity to shift the needle of the said emblematic clock
sufficiently back towards safety.

SUMIT CHOWDHURY (On Amazon)

SWITCHED ON

``This is the book we have been waiting for. It is a significant
attempt towards developing a better understanding of the
Deep State of America, and that of many other countries.
These Deep States are able to stage-manage nearly every war
on the planet Earth in a way that ensures business as usual for
their vast military industrial complexes. Together, these Deep
States are all set to create war fronts at several locations on
the planet, never mind if the common people of these warring

countries do not want war. The author makes a valiant attempt to awaken the conscience and common sense of the human beings so that we can `dismantle` these Deep States of the World and reach a new stage in our lives where we can look back on war as an incomprehensible aberration of our past``

Prof. M.S.Swaminathan ..Founder Chairman and Chief Mentor UNESCO Chair in Eco Technology. M.S.Swaminathan Research Foundation. Ex-President Pugwash Conferences on Science and World Affairs.

``At the outset, I wish to mention that Sagar`s latest book unlike his previous books (stressing on the scientific aspects of cosmology and the place of mind in the universe) concentrates on the geopolitics of "Deep States" and "Military Industrial complex (MIC)" in the US in particular and in other nations in general. The first half of the full text explains how the Deep States and MIC work in parallel to national governments to thwart all efforts by all concerned to bring about peaceful resolution of all intra- and international civil, political, social, economic, ethno-religious -ecological and other conflicts. What is more, they indeed acerbate such conflicts to such a pitch as to increase the danger of nuclear warfare or ecological Armageddon in the near future to near certainty. In particular, the Deep States and MIC of the US, Russia and China enhance the risk of nuclear war far more than those of other nations. This endangers the continued survival and evolution of mind alone not only alone on earth but prevents the opportunity near at hand for mind on earth to integrate with and ride piggy-back on a universe-wide mind possibly in existence at a higher stage of evolution than ours.

The second half of the text tries to find solution to the problems created by the Deep States and MIC so that the mind on earth is freed to evolve along its path in a smooth and uncluttered manner. Sagar`s bringing in the whole text in the style of Greek dialogues between "revised versions" or reincarnations of path-breaking scientists and philosophers of the past tries to add spice to the issues under discussion without in any way allowing the seriousness of the discussion to sag in any way. The conclusions though fuzzy cannot but be otherwise in an attempt to read and if possible, alter the future of humanity and the universal mind towards its best glory. If this book during its publication could reach leaders of all the nuclear nations and nations with vast MICs and the representatives of all other member nations of the UNGA, one hopes there is a chance, however slender, that the earth-wide mind is set on its evolutionary path towards uncluttered improvement to its fullest potential. This chance singularly justifies all his painstaking efforts in bringing out the book. I wish all success to the book while hoping it has the widest possible reach among those who are concerned about peace and progress on earth as also among those who wittingly or unwittingly are threats to such peace and progress so that both their minds are reoriented to merge and move together in unison from here onwards.``

A.K.Chandrashekhar .. Retired Finance Executive with interest in Science, Philosophy, and social well being.

In appreciation of the Scientists of the
Pugwash Group and the Authors of the
`Bulletin of Atomic Scientists`

INTRODUCTION

If 'This' happens, then 'That' is likely to happen and if 'That' is not good for the world, then 'This' should not be allowed to happen.

Something happened in California in early November 2015, where people saw a mysterious bright light in the sky. It was a direct consequence of Einstein's Special Relativity Theory. A lot of things are happening, which are all a direct consequence of Einstein's theories.

To better understand the laws of science, scientist Lee Smolin suggests we should regard quantum theory as the record of quantum information that one subsystem may have about another subsystem as a result of their mutual interaction. In other words, the universe - as suggested by scientist Seth Lloyd - can be considered to be a quantum computer. One may ask the question, "But what does the universe compute?" Lloyd gives the answer, "It computes its own behavior. At first, the patterns it produces are simple, but as it processes more and more information, the patterns produced are more intricate and complex. On the physical side, this gives rise to galaxies, stars, and planets while on the human side, it produces life - human beings, society, language and culture."

My own idea is that all this takes place in a field. When enough information is accumulated within this field, it becomes an intelligent field. The intelligence in this field keeps increasing and like the capacity of an infinite mind, it focuses on creating biochemistries suitable for generating awareness and consciousness to understand itself.

So, it boils down to this - it is the information in this field that is responsible for what happens in reality. This reality then becomes the information that is responsible for what happens next. Hence, it can be said that information creates reality, which creates information, which creates reality, and so on. The complexities keep rising all the time.

In this book, I provide information on what has been happening on planet Earth since the beginning of the 20th century. This 'Information in the Field', is relayed as transmitted to my brain by the interactions of the world on me.

So, I place all my cards on the table, make some assumptions, do some calculations, and arrive at some conclusions on what lies ahead for the human race - what are our chances of winning the game of survival versus extinction; if good sense does not prevail.

And what does extinction mean?

Simply this: All the billions of souls (currently about 7.5 billion) come out in the open, into the atmosphere or maybe stranded in interstellar space, with no biochemistry available on planet Earth to get back into human consciousness again.

Finally, I give my humble views on what can be that 'good sense' which can save us from extinction.

So, if it turns out that great leaders of nations that matter, some day assemble in a conference with the primary aim of saving humanity from nuclear self-destruction, they should arrive at the conference with an unbiased approach and a neutral perspective. They should not consider themselves representatives of a nation or religion. They should be members of a team of experts, completely focused in first understanding the problems, and then adopting an integrated approach to resolving those problems. Above all, they should be well prepared and in possession of all the 'Information in the Field' as provided in this book.

Never mind the source of all the information and the extent to which extracts from these sources have been utilised. This was necessary to make the story crisp, interesting, engaging and a reflection of the contemporary state of affairs on this subject. I am convinced that these will add an element of relevance and interest for the reader who cares about the matters of the world. I have adequately and appropriately referenced these.

Three of the chapters (Three, Five, and Six) are on Science and Philosophy, leading to the development of a model of philosophy that has the best chance of finding global acceptance. This can pave the way towards uniting the world's religions into a single religion whose essence is nothing but 'Peaceful Coexistence' and 'To Live and Let Live'.

The present book and my two earlier ones 'SIX WORDS' and 'INTELLIGENT FIELD' have similar objectives. On a broad level, the idea is to develop a model of philosophy that looks at the possibility of an existential truth, which can ultimately bind the universe together; a model of philosophy that has the best chance of finding acceptance worldwide. All the three books are essentially Mind and Consciousness Studies. All three of them explain how and why the universe is obliged to make sense and provide a unity of consciousness that ensures a bright future for life in general, including life on planet Earth. All three books discuss - in varying levels of detail - about the Nuclear Geopolitics of the world, and the dangers humans face due to the impending nuclear wars that threaten the continued existence of mankind in a big way. And finally, all three books are in-depth explorations into how humans can come together to change the course of history.

Nevertheless, each of the three books has a certain 'Specialness' to it that is explained below:

In 'SIX WORDS' which I treat as my autobiography, I arrive in the universe as a quark during the first second of the big bang, progress to become an atom of Hydrogen. My journey through the cosmos, then leads me to a star about to die. The star becomes a Supernova, and in the process of nucleosynthesis, I am converted into a carbon atom and explode out of the star. After God knows how many millions of years, I arrive on planet Earth. On Earth I become an organic molecule, perhaps equipped with a soul. Then again, after God knows how many millions of years and countless varieties of lives, I finally become a Structural Engineer. Through this process, I explain the salient aspects of Cosmology to the readers in simple language.

My autobiography continues. I read a large number of books on Quantum Physics and Cosmology and get foxed. I get confused with complexities such as Non-Objectivity,

Observer Created Realities, Particle Wave Duality, The Collapse of the Wave Function, The Probability Wave, and above all the non-local action, that Entanglement and so on. So confusing! I then get philosophical - what else could I do. Then I get some ideas - can't call them visions.

And finally, there is a breakthrough. The SIX WORDS strike me. And with that striking blow comes the idea that I should write a book.

So, one Saturday morning after breakfast, with two expected rounds of coffee and Rachmaninoff's Piano Concerto No. 3 playing on the music system, I compose a full chapter - all of forty odd pages - on Quantum Entanglement. I explain to the readers a complete story of the sequential development of the science of Quantum Physics, as it happened over the years. Finally, I discuss the philosophical impact of Quantum Physics that led to Six Words.

So far, it's a true story, and then I get invited to an imaginary seminar. We can call it a 'Seminar held in a Parallel Universe', where great Scientists and Philosophers of the World - some of them revised versions of the original men and women - come together to provide their inputs and give their presentations. Einstein talks about his 'Cosmic Religious Feelings', Schrodinger and Sherrington talk about the 'Oneness of the Mind' and describe the 'Flickering Light Thought Experiment' in support of their concept. John Wheeler with his 'Law without Law' and 'The Participating Observer', Eugene Wigner with his idea that it is the consciousness of the observer that collapses the wave function, Immanuel Kant with his 'Unity of Consciousness', Descartes with his words 'I think therefore I am', Amaury De

Riencourt and 'Squaring the Circle - Beyond the Mind' Paul Davies with his profound idea that 'God is a Mind' and many others.

A model of philosophy is then developed, which encapsulates the ideas of all the speakers who gave presentations. At the center of this model of philosophy, are the 'SIX WORDS'.

In 'INTELLIGENT FIELD' the specialness increases several folds. The central theme is the idea of a Travelling Cosmic Mind that can travel not just in Space, but also in Time. In this way, it somehow manages to remain forever in an era where galaxies are forming, stars are shining, where life and consciousness is flourishing at millions of locations in the universe. The 'TCM' does not have to proceed to the non-livable eras of deep future - which are trillions and trillions of times longer lasting than the livable eras - as it cannot obtain consciousness there. In principle, this is just about the only way the universe can make sense to the thinking mind.

The subject of Einstein's relativity theories, is discussed threadbare and it is shown how the idea of the 'TCM' is in complete consonance with Einstein's Relativity Principle (ERP). It adequately explains all the various 'Causality Violation Paradoxes' which ensue as a consequence of ERP. It is strong, intelligent and will keep producing islands of negative entropy for lives and consciousnesses to flourish and understand the universe; not just for a while, but for all times to come. Without it, the arrow of time will always point to the dissolution of structure into a featureless state of maximum entropy. Indeed, the traveling cosmic mind comes to our rescue and saves us from that bleak future.

It explains the concept of Quantum Entanglement perfectly. The mere fact that there is such a thing as Quantum Entanglement implies instant connectivity. This connectivity is impossible to imagine, except by the consideration of an omnipresent mind (omnipresent in time as well as space).

A section in 'Intelligent Field in Time' explains in simple language the 'Speculative Theories of the Early Universe' as well as of 'Degenerate, Black-Hole and Dark Eras of Deep Future' elaborately.

The model of philosophy as worked out in 'Six Words' is strengthened further with the idea of an 'Intelligent Field' and 'The Travelling Cosmic Mind' as described in the book. This has added a significantly new dimension to the quest for knowledge on Philosophy, Religion, Spirituality, Humanism, and other similar paths towards formulating an integrative view of Life and the Universe.

There is also an in-depth and lengthy discussion - to our heart's content - on 'Mind, Body and Soul', the philosophy of 'Six Words', as well as on Schrodinger's 'Flickering Light Thought' experiment, along with the linkage of these subjects with the ideas of 'Intelligent Field' and the 'TCM'. Some people agree, some disagree while others have advised me to be more pragmatic in my approach, and not be too excited about the travelling cosmic mind (the travelling part in particular). Some have said that all these ideas will remain unverifiable until our present limited consciousness evolves ultimately into an infinite mind (IM). However, all agree with the idea that the mind and consciousness have a central place in the ultimate nature of reality; never mind whether the said idea is not professionally useful to contemporary scientists, or practically useful to build machines. It can be philosophically useful to unite science with religion, to unite people, cultures and religions, to end conflicts and wars, and so on.

Coming now to the present book 'Bright Light In The Sky'. The specialty of this book lies in its coverage of the Nuclear Geopolitics of the World. It is far more comprehensive and elaborate than `Intelligent Field', which in turn is far more elaborate than 'Six Words'. It is also more up-to-date; as close as possible to the month of publication. In fact, the primary reason for writing this third book - so soon after the second one - is the sudden and sharp deterioration in the world situation. As a result of this, the 'Bulletin of Atomic Scientists' have shifted the needle of the Doomsday Emblematic Clock from 3 minutes to midnight, to as close as 2 minutes to midnight.

In brief, the subject matter of the book is as follows:

The title 'Bright Light in The Sky' pertains to a Nuclear Test carried out at California, USA, in early November 2015. The book features the complete sequence of events relating to the Nuclear Geopolitics of the World starting with Einstein's equations and the discovery of fission, right up to the end of the year 2018. The highlight of the book is the development of a mathematical relationship between the location of the needle of the 'Doomsday Emblematic Clock' as periodically worked out by the authors of the journal 'The Bulletin of Atomic Scientists', and the probability of a nuclear attack taking place anywhere on planet Earth in one year. Based on this empirical relation and some other parameters, what lies ahead for the human race has been worked out in mathematical terms - if good sense remains elusive.

And what exactly is the 'Good Sense' that can save us from 'Extinction'? This is captured and explained in simple language in one of the chapters of this book.

The philosophical model is strengthened still further with the idea that our universe could be a Simulated Universe, a kind of Quantum Computer that in fact computes its own behaviour.

In one of the chapters titled 'SWITCHED ON - Arguments for and against Simulation', the subject of 'Simulation' is discussed threadbare. In fact, it is a reproduction of an actual discussion that took place in response to a blog on Huffington Post. This discussion was initiated by 'Yours Truly' who was one of the three members who participated in the same.

Notwithstanding the fact that at the current level of our understanding, it is impossible to establish the number of aeons that preceded the current aeon of the universe. The manner in which Simulation took place, and under what mechanism could the constants of nature have been implanted in the system that 'Switched On' the big bang? The fact remains that the operation was hugely successful in creating an Eternal and Everlasting Universe with life and consciousness evolving and flourishing in the galaxies.

Simulation or no simulation, we are now in a Universe which can last forever, where life and consciousness are evolving and flourishing in the galaxies. The livable era is however unlikely to last beyond a certain length of time which is but an insignificant part of the total life of the universe.

All that is required now is to establish how the universe can make sense, and what can that philosophical model be, so as to ensure permanent consciousness for us all.

Which is what I have endeavoured to do in my books 'Six Words', 'Intelligent Field' and 'Bright Light In The Sky'.

CONTENTS

Chapter One
Information In The Field

BRIGHT LIGHT IN THE SKY

As reported by BBC, sometime in early November 2015, people in California saw a mysterious bright light in the sky. The flare rose high in the air and a wide, bright blue flash emerged in the shape of a cone. The display could be seen for several minutes. Pretty soon videos were posted online and this sent the Californians into panic.

Social media was flooded with theories and people were asking questions. Was it a comet or a meteor, a nuclear missile attack or a nuclear bomb? Some people knew that a day prior to this phenomenon, the Federal Aviation Authorities had issued flight restrictions to the LA International Airport, denying aircraft access to one of the most frequent approach paths for international and domestic travel.

The official explanation given soon after was that the US Navy had launched a test missile as a 'routine' test.

Why was that necessary?
What in the world is going on?
What is the real story behind all this?
I will now go back a little over a hundred years, to the beginning of the story, the beginning of the sequence of events that led to the said nuclear test.

To begin with, I believe that it is the information in the field that is responsible for what happens in reality. This reality then becomes the information that is responsible for what happens next. Hence, it can be said that information creates reality, which creates information, which creates reality, and so on. The complexities keep rising all the time.

Sometimes, the information is planned, and consequently what happens is more or less on expected lines, depending upon the quality of the plan and its execution. An example of this would be - first design a tall reinforced concrete structure to withstand the forces of nature and the anticipated imposed loads on it. After which, one needs to erect the building with quality construction, in accordance with the design and drawings as planned.

At times, there is no plan and randomness just creeps in, resulting in all sorts of chaotic things.

Sometimes (almost always), a combination of planned information and random information - which in turn can be a planned information from another sequence - interfere in a chaotic manner, leading ultimately to innumerable other sequences completely unforeseen by any of the planners.

Having said that, I hereby place all the cards on the table, all the information in the field on what happened in the past, beginning with Einstein's equation and continuing to the present day - whether positive or negative - in the interest of peace. All of this has had some bearing on our current situation. We have about twenty thousand nuclear warheads located at several locations on the planet; not all of them are in safe hands.

EINSTEIN'S EQUATION AND THE DISCOVERY OF FISSION

It all began with Einstein's special relativity theory. The understanding of the equivalence of mass and energy, and of course the equation $E=mc^2$. This equation implied that even something of a very small mass had the potential of creating a huge amount of energy, that has enormously far reaching significance. The ball was set to roll for experimental research on the subject. Scientists and science fiction writers started imagining the consequences of utilising this energy that is released in radioactivity. H.G. Wells, author of the famous "TIME MACHINE", wrote a book titled "THE WORLD SET FREE", wherein the words 'atomic bombs' were used for the very first time. Politicians and World Leaders started predicting the future war scenarios. In November 1931, Winston Churchill wrote:

"It would be much better to call a halt in material progress and (scientific) discovery, rather than to be mastered by our own apparatus and the forces which it directs."

Then, in March 1934, Churchill wrote:

"In the fires of Science, burning with increasing heat every year, all the most dearly loved conventions are being melted down; and this is a process which is going to continually increase."

But Einstein himself did not show any concern - perhaps deliberately - to avoid panic about the possibility of harnessing energy from atomic nuclei. When an interviewer specifically asked him about such a possibility, Einstein replied:

"I feel absolutely sure, nearly sure, that it will not be possible; it will be like shooting birds in the dark, in a country where there are few birds."

One scientist however was telling anyone who would listen that Einstein was wrong; that nuclear weapons were a distinct possibility. And that scientist was 'Leo Szilard'.

'To tell Leo Szilard that something cannot be done was to spur him on a crisp refutation. He liked nothing better than to disprove dogmas and to shock everyone with his boldness and ingenuity. In this way, he came to be the first to outline how nuclear energy might

be harnessed, possibly to make bombs, and to warn that such weapons might soon be in the hands of tyrants', said Churchill, in Graham Farmelo's book "Churchill's Bomb".

Again, in November 1937, Churchill wrote:

"In the next fifty years, mankind will make greater progress in mastering and applying greater forces than in the last million years or more. This is a fearsome thought. And the first question we must ask ourselves is, are we fit for it? Are we worthy of all these exalted responsibilities? Can we bear this tremendous strain?"
Churchill wrote several essays on the subject including "Shall we all commit suicide?" In one of these he wrote:

"There is no question amongst scientists that this gigantic source of energy exists. What is lacking is the match to set the bonfire alight."
(1A -01)

And then, in early January 1939, the 'match' that would one day 'light that fire' was found during a walk in the woods.

A certain walk in the snow-covered woods outside Stockholm, shaped the future of humans. It was a walk during which scientists Lise Meitner and her nephew Otto Frisch, discussed the findings of the experimental research carried out by another scientist, Otto Hahn. During this discussion, they discerned something of extreme significance related to the splitting of the uranium nucleus and its consequent release of energy.

Otto Frisch recalled in his memoirs (1A-01A) later, how puzzled Lise Meitner was while studying a letter from Hahn. When he read the letter and understood its significance, their walk in the snowy woods changed the way they looked at the world. The revelations before them in that letter, about the three substances being barium and not radium, led gradually to the idea that:

"This was no chipping or cracking of the nucleus, but rather a process to be explained by Bohr's idea that the nucleus is like a liquid drop; such a drop might elongate and divide itself. We knew that there were strong forces that would resist such a process - just as the surface tension of an ordinary liquid drop resists its division into two smaller ones. But nuclei differed from ordinary drops in one important way: they were electrically charged, and this was known to diminish the effect of the surface tension."

Some calculations hurriedly performed on scraps of paper that fateful day, revealed that the charge of the Uranium Nucleus was large enough to destroy the effect of surface tension almost completely. In fact, the Uranium Nucleus might be unstable and ready to divide itself at the slightest provocation - like an impact, say, from a neutron.

The problem that was attached to this seemingly simple split of the Uranium Nucleus was that they could be driven apart by their mutual electric repulsion and would acquire a very large energy of almost 200 MeV.

Lise Meitner had at this point, using the packing fraction formula, worked out that the sum of the parts of the masses of two resultant nuclei would be about one-fifth of the mass of a proton short. Whenever mass disappears like this, energy is created and as per the mass energy equivalence relationship, $E=mc^2$, one-fifth of the mass of the proton was nothing but 200 MeV. As this seemed to just about fit, the revelation loomed large upon them - unlimited prospects towards achievement of energy security for the world. What was not very apparent at that time, however, was that this singular event was instrumental perhaps, in taking us a step closer toward the collapse of civilization.

THE RACE FOR SUPREMACY AND EINSTEIN'S LETTERS TO PRESIDENT ROOSEVELT

The properties of uranium, the nuclear chain reaction, and the findings that such a chain reaction could either be controlled to produce usable energy, or be allowed to go out of control to produce a violent explosion, led scientists worldwide to undertake experiments on the subject.

Two letters written by Einstein to President Roosevelt in August 1939 and March 1940 (the latter actually written to Dr. Alexander Sachs for onward transmission to Roosevelt), warning them of the German research in fission, and urging the President to initiate and speed up a research program in the United States to explore the feasibility of atomic bombs, were considered by many as the biggest and most powerful interactions between Einstein and the United States. The German occupation of Czechoslovakia had brought a halt to the sale of uranium, and evidence pointed to intensive nuclear research by German scientists. The two letters, along with a third letter that resulted in the start of the Manhattan Project (contents reproduced below), contributed significantly toward enormous atomic research efforts in the United States, that ultimately tilted the scales in favour of the United States in the race towards the use of the first atomic bomb.

Contents of the third letter (in part):

"I am convinced as to the wisdom and the urgency of creating the conditions under which that and related work [referring to the research work of Szilard and Wigner] can be carried out with greater speed and on a larger scale than hitherto. I was interested in a suggestion made by Dr. Sachs that the Special Advisory Committee supply names of persons to serve as a board of trustees for a nonprofit organization, which with the approval of the government committee, could secure from governmental or private sources or both, the necessary funds for carrying out the work. Given such a framework and the necessary funds, it [the large-scale experiments and exploration of practical applications] could be carried out much faster than through a loose cooperation of university laboratories and government departments." (1A-02 and 1A-03)

THE MANHATTAN PROJECT

The "non-profit organization" refers of course, to the organization responsible for carrying out the Manhattan Project. The letter was implemented briskly. The Briggs Committee was drastically re-organised and brought under the wing of the National Defense Research Committee created by Roosevelt. A special committee of the National Academy of Sciences was set up to inform the government of any development in nuclear fission that might affect defence.

Though Einstein was an out-and-out pacifist, there was no way he could have not written these letters, as the consequence of the Germans first using an atomic bomb might have been catastrophic. Had these letters not been written, we have no idea what the history of the planet would have been for the past seventy years. More than 130,000 people worked on the Manhattan Project. The total cost of the project was in excess of 2 billion US dollars. It was operated entirely under a shroud of secrecy, so much so that President Harry S. Truman, who took over the presidency upon Roosevelt's death in April 1945, had no prior knowledge of the same.

THE BOMBING OF HIROSHIMA AND NAGASAKI AND THE AFTERMATH

On December 17, 1944, Lieutenant Colonel Paul W. Tibbets Jr. was given command of the newly created 509th Composite Group of the Army-Air Force. Its top-secret mission was to drop the world's first atomic bomb. The unique shapes of the "Little Boy" and "Fat Man" bombs required a great deal of testing with pumpkin bombs to ensure an accurate flight on being dropped from specially modified B-29 planes. The 509th trained at a scheduled base in Wendover before being sent to Tinian Island in the Marianas in May, June, and July of 1945. At Tinian, the Manhattan Project recreated a "Little Manhattan," naming the roads after New York City streets. *(1A-04)*

The mission of the 509th was a secret so well kept that Admiral Chester W. Nimitz, Commander-in-Chief of the Pacific theatre, did not know of the atomic bomb until February 1945. A target committee was convened in April and May 1945 to short list Japanese cities as possible atomic bomb candidates. By the end of July, the list included Hiroshima, Kokura, Niigata and Nagasaki. Former Secretary of War, Harry Simpson, vetoed the ancient capital of Kyoto due to its magnificent shrines and temples. On July 25 1945, official orders were issued to the 509th Composite Group to deliver its first atomic bomb as soon as the weather permitted visual bombing after about August 3, 1945, on one of the targets. Additional bombs were delivered on the targets mentioned above as soon as they were readied by the project staff. The order was issued to General Carl Spaatz, Commanding General of the US Army Strategic Air Forces, with the directive that the discussion of any and all information concerning the use of the weapon against Japan was reserved for the Secretary of War and the President of the United States. It was signed by Thomas T. Handy, General GSC, acting Chief-of-Staff. General Spaatz was directed to personally deliver a copy to General MacArthur and another to Admiral Nimitz.

At 0245 Tinian time on Monday, August 6, 1945, Colonel Tibbets and his crew took off in the Enola Gay. As the crew approached the mainland of Japan, the weather was clear for the visual drop requirement. Colonel Tibbets described the final minutes before the drop:

"We made the final turn to 272 degrees' magnetic course for fourteen minutes (72NM). Major Ferebee (group bombardier) checked the bombing sights and said, 'I have the aiming point in sight.' Captain Van Kirk (navigator) checked and agreed. The crew put on dark goggles and turned on the tone for the instrument plane to know exactly when the bomb was released. Two small corrections were made, and we finally released the bomb."

At precisely seventeen seconds after 0815 (Japan time), the Enola Gay released the first atomic bomb over the target of Hiroshima.

"Little Boy" fell from 31,600 feet, detonating forty-three seconds later, six hundred yards in the air over the city. In a millisecond, a force of twenty thousand tons of TNT was released, generating a fireball of heat equivalent to three hundred thousand degrees Fahrenheit. The temperature on the ground beneath the burst reached an estimated three thousand to four thousand degrees Centigrade, and the heat rays caused flesh burns up to thirteen thousand feet away. Nearly eighty thousand people were killed instantly, and almost every building within a two-mile radius was obliterated.

Historian Tsuyoshi Hasegawa, describes the utter devastation of the bomb in Japan in complete contrast to the sense of overwhelming success in Washington DC, as President Truman warned the Japanese to 'expect a rain of ruin'.

As per his account, "Little Boy" exploded 1900 feet above the courtyard of Shima Hospital, 550 feet off its target, Aioi Bridge over Ota River, with a yield equivalent to 12,500 tons of TNT. The temperature at ground zero reached 5400 degrees Fahrenheit. An image of the aftermath would relay destruction of a scale unimaginable. With a statistic of 76,000 buildings in Hiroshima; 70,000 were destroyed, and the death toll totaled to 1,40,000 by the end of 1945. The way so many met their painful end differed. The instant fireball right after the blast charred everyone within half a mile as their internal organs boiled. People were instantly pulverised leaving behind what are called 'Nuclear' shadows. The fire that broke out in the city devoured everything in its path leading to a slew of charred bodies everywhere. Thousands floated in the river while others were strewn on the streets. People walked aimlessly in eerie silence or haplessly ran about looking for their dear ones, many black with burns, their skin peeling. Black rain followed, soaking everyone in radiation. Whoever the initial shock couldn't kill, began dying of radiation sickness.

When a report with the message, "Big bomb dropped on Hiroshima" was handed over to President Truman by Captain Frank Graham of the White House Map Room, the President beamed. He jumped to his feet and shook hands with Graham. "Captain," he said, "this is the greatest thing in history."

In a broadcast that evening, Don Goddard compared the instant destruction at Hiroshima to an entire city like Denver, Colorado housing 350,000; there one moment and wiped out the other.

President Truman issued a statement immediately after the world's first atomic bomb was dropped on Hiroshima. His statement unveiled the Manhattan Project as an immense "scientific gamble" and the "greatest achievement of organised science in history." Looking ahead, President Truman envisioned the production and use of atomic energy for power within the United States and as a force for maintaining world peace. *(1A-04)*

The Manhattan Project was successful; it was an "unsurpassed accomplishment of Science and an Engineering feat." The United States won the race for the first use of the atomic bomb. On August 14, 1945, Japan surrendered unconditionally. The Second World War ended.

THE DOOMSDAY EMBLEMATIC CLOCK

In 1947, a couple of years after the Hiroshima and Nagasaki Nuclear attacks that signalled the end of World War II, the Bulletin of Atomic Scientists evolved from a newsletter into a magazine, and the Clock appeared on the cover for the first time. It symbolised the urgency of the nuclear dangers that the magazine's founders and the broader scientific community were trying to convey to the public and political leaders around the world. The clock was called the 'Doomsday Emblematic Clock.'

In 1947, the clock stood at 7 minutes to midnight.

In 1949, President Harry Truman told the American public that the Soviets had tested their first nuclear device, officially starting in the arms race. "We do not advise Americans that doomsday is near and that they can expect atomic bombs to start falling on their heads a month or year from now," the Bulletin explained. "But we think they have reason to be deeply alarmed and to be prepared for grave decisions."

The clock was moved by four minutes; from 7 minutes to 3 minutes to midnight.

In 1950 after much debate, the United States decided to pursue the hydrogen bomb, a weapon far more powerful than any atomic bomb. On 1st November 1952, the United States tested their first thermonuclear device, obliterating a Pacific Ocean islet in the process. Nine months later, the Soviets tested an H-bomb of their own. "The hands of the Clock of Doom have moved again," the Bulletin announced. "Only a few more swings of the pendulum and from Moscow to Chicago, atomic explosions will strike midnight for western civilization."

The clock stood at **2** minutes to midnight.

Over the years, depending on the seriousness - or otherwise - of the situation, the clock moved 'closer' or 'away' from midnight. Complete record of the Movement of the 'Doomsday Emblematic Clock' from 1947 to the present date will be furnished in this chapter.

NUCLEAR ARMS RACE

Frantic build-up of nuclear capabilities by powerful nations of the world was a natural consequence, as was the urgency to ensure control of such a build-up by other nations. The Non Proliferation Treaty, The Comprehensive Test Ban Treaty, and The International Atomic Energy Act, all expounded upon the safeguards necessary to ensure that nuclear material does not go into the wrong hands. The Atomic Energy Act of 1954 (section 123 of the act pertains to cooperation with other nations), talked about the demand - supply gap in energy, the necessity for more and more nations in the world to partake in the responsibility to ensure prevention of use of nuclear weapons, and so forth.

PUGWASH CONFERENCES AND THE RUSSELL / EINSTEIN MANIFESTO *(1A-05)*

The Pugwash conferences got their name from the fishing village of Pugwash, Nova Scotia. The first meeting was held in 1957, and was attended by twenty-two eminent scientists (seven from the United States, three each from the Soviet Union and Japan, two each from the United Kingdom and Canada, and one each from Australia, Austria, China, France, and Poland). The stimulus for the first Pugwash meeting was the manifesto issued in 1955 by Bertrand Russell and Albert Einstein. It was also signed by Max Born, Percy Bridgman, Leopold Infeld, Frederic Joliot-Curie, Herman Muller, Linus Pauling, Cecil Powell, Joseph Rotblat, and Hideki Yukawa. It called upon scientists of all political persuasions to assemble in order to discuss the threat posed to civilization by the advent of thermonuclear weapons.

This is an extract from the Russell/Einstein manifesto *(1A-04A)*:

"In the tragic situation that confronts humanity, we feel that scientists should assemble in the conference to appraise the perils that have arisen as a result of the development of weapons of mass destruction, and to discuss a resolution in the spirit of the appended draft.

We are speaking on this occasion, not as members of any nation, continent or creed, but as human beings, as members of the species Man - whose continued existence is in doubt. The world is full of conflicts, and overshadowing all minor conflicts is the titanic struggle between communism and anticommunism.

Almost everybody who is politically conscious, has strong feelings about one or more of these issues, but we want you - if you can - to set aside such feelings and consider yourselves only as members of a biological species that has had a remarkable history, whose disappearance none of us desire.

We shall try not to say a single word that would appeal to just one group and not to another. All are equally in peril and if this peril is understood, there is hope that they may collectively avert it.

We need to learn to think in a new way. We must learn to ask ourselves not what steps can be taken to give military victory to whatever group we prefer; for there no longer are such choices. The question we need to ask ourselves here is: what steps can be taken to prevent a military contest, the result of which would be equally disastrous to all parties.

It is stated on very good authority that a bomb can now be manufactured which will be 2,500 times more powerful than the one that destroyed Hiroshima. Such a bomb, if exploded near the ground or under water, sends radioactive particles into the upper air. No one knows how widely such lethal radioactive particles might be diffused, but the best authorities are unanimous in saying that a war with hydrogen bombs might possibly put an end to the human race. It is feared that if multiple hydrogen bombs are triggered, there will be universal death. While this may be sudden death only for a minority, for a majority it will be a slow torture of disease and disintegration.

Most of us are not neutral in feeling, but as human beings, we have to remember; if the issues between the East and the West are to be decided in a manner that can satisfy everybody - whether a communist or an anti-communist, whether an Asian, European or American, whether white or black - then these issues must not be decided by war. We should wish this to be understood, both in the East and the West.

Continuous progress in happiness, knowledge and wisdom lies before us, only if we choose it. Shall we instead choose death because we cannot forget our quarrels? We appeal as human beings to human beings: remember your humanity and forget the rest. If you can do so, the way to a new paradise lies open to you. If you cannot, there lies before you the risk of universal death.

Resolution: We invite this congress and through it the scientists of the world and the public in general, to subscribe to the following resolution:

In view of the fact that in any future world war, nuclear weapons will certainly be engaged, and that such weapons threaten the continued existence of mankind; we urge the governments of the world to realise, and to acknowledge publicly, that their purpose cannot be furthered by a world war. We urge them to consequently find peaceful means for the settlement of all matters of dispute between them."

The 1957 meeting was hosted by the American Philanthropist Cyrus Eaton, in his birthplace at the Thinkers' Lodge in Pugwash. Eaton continued to provide crucial support for the conferences in their early years.

From the beginning, there evolved both a continuing series of meetings at locations all over the world with a growing number and diversity of participants, along with a decentralised organizational structure to coordinate and finance this activity. By September 2002, there had been over 275 Pugwash conferences, symposia, and workshops, with a total attendance of over four thousand scientists and other individuals.

Pugwash conducts between eight to twelve meetings a year, including a large annual conference, attended by 150 to 250 people. The more frequent workshops and study group meetings that focus on specific issues, typically involve twenty to fifty participants. A basic rule is that participation always comes from individuals in their private capacities (not as representatives of governments or organizations).

Here is an extract from the website of Pugwash Conferences from the section 'ABOUT PUGWASH':

44

"The purpose of the Pugwash Conference is to bring together influential scientists, scholars and public figures from around the world, who are concerned about reducing the danger of armed conflict and our seeking cooperative solutions for global problems. Meeting in private as individuals rather than as representatives of governments or institutions, the participants of Pugwash Conferences exchange views and explore alternative approaches towards arms control and tension reduction. This is done with a flexibility seldom attained in official East-West and North-South discussions or negotiations. Yet, because of the stature of many of the Pugwash participants in their own countries (for example science and arms control advisers to governments, key figures in academies of science and universities, and former or future holders of high government office), insights from Pugwash discussions tend to penetrate quickly to the appropriate levels of official policymaking.

The first two decades of Pugwash coincided with some of the most dangerous years of the Cold War, marked by the Berlin Crisis, the Cuban Missile Crisis, the Repression of the Prague Spring in Czechoslovakia, and the Vietnam War. In this period of strained official relations and a few unofficial channels, the fora and lines of communication provided by Pugwash played useful background roles in helping lay the groundwork for the Partial Test Ban Treaty of 1963, the Nonproliferation Treaty of 1968, the Antiballistic Missile Treaty of 1972, the SALT I accords, the Biological Weapons Convention of 1972, the Intermediate-Range Theatre Nuclear Force (INF) Treaty, as well as the Chemical Weapons Convention of 1993.

Despite subsequent trends of generally improving East-West relations, and the emergence of a much wider array of unofficial channels of communication, Pugwash meetings have continued to play an important role in bringing together key scientists, analysts and policy advisers for sustained, in-depth discussions of the crucial arms control issues of the day, particularly in the areas of nuclear, chemical and biological weapons."

JOSEPH ROTBLAT

Joseph Rotblat was the main driving force behind the Pugwash movement. A nuclear scientist par excellence, he worked on the Manhattan Project but left amid controversial circumstances.

As Andrew Brown, the author of the book 'Keeper of the Nuclear Conscience' writes, "The subsequent bombings of Hiroshima and Nagasaki intensified his (Rotblat's) ethical concern over the involvement of scientists in developing weapons of mass destruction and drove him to become deeply involved in the anti-war movement."

Brown tells the story of Rotblat, who dedicated his life to the furtherance of peace among nations and above all, the prevention of nuclear wars. It is also the story of a time of intense superpower rivalry and a time when scientists had the ears of presidents and premiers.

MY AMAZON.COM REVIEW OF THE BOOK "KEEPER OF THE NUCLEAR CONSCIENCE" BY ANDREW BROWN

"It is better for peace in the world if this is widely read. Andrew Brown has written a masterpiece about the life and times of Joseph Rotblat, a nuclear scientist par excellence. His brilliance was demonstrated even more in making the scientists of his time understand their responsibilities and leading them to play vital roles in launching an ethical revolution. Rotblat dedicated his life to the furtherance of peace among nations and above all, the prevention of nuclear wars. He was the main driving force behind the Pugwash movement (the conferences) that brought together influential scientists, scholars, and public figures from around the world, who were concerned with the danger of armed conflicts, and wanted to seek solutions for global problems. The stimulus for these conferences was provided by a manifesto issued by Albert Einstein and Bertrand Russell in 1955.

The book is a historical review of events of the twentieth century (not necessarily described in a sequential way), with all the essential information. The author has placed all the cards on the table about what happened in the past. How many times in the past has the emblematic clock moved closer to midnight just minutes before the pressing of the nuclear buttons? How were the probabilities to prevent the pressing of those buttons created?

Books like these should be in private libraries of leaders of nations. No harm would be done if these leaders partook in the Pugwash movement, not as members of this or that nation, religion or creed, but as human beings whose continued existence is in doubt. As Einstein and Russell stated in their manifesto, they should consider themselves members of a biological species which has had a remarkable history, and whose disappearance none of us can would desire."

THE 1962 CUBAN MISSILE CRISIS AND ITS AFTERMATH

As described by James Martin in his book 'Meaning of the 21st Century':

"The world came shockingly close to a nuclear war in 1962 with the Cuban Missile Crisis. In the defining moments of this crisis, the United States blockaded a Soviet fleet to prevent it from going to Cuba. The executive committee of the United States, who called the shots, was unaware that the four Soviet submarines had nuclear weapons. At about 5 pm on October 27, 1962, an American ship depth-charged a Soviet submarine, unaware that it had a nuclear weapon on board. The depth-charge exploded next to the hull but didn't penetrate it. The Russian captain felt honour-bound to retaliate and ordered for a nuclear weapon to be launched at the Americans. In order to do so, two other officers had to agree to fire and turn their keys simultaneously. At the last moment, the second captain, Vasili Alexandrovich Arkhipov, refused. Had he not done so, the result would have been a devastating nuclear war.

In the 1980s, the game sped up drastically. Cruise missiles, designed to carry nuclear warheads vastly more powerful than the

47

Hiroshima bomb, were built. The nuclear command and control systems were designed so that the nuclear retaliation would happen automatically with preprogrammed missiles, at the highest level of alert. The situation became like that of the gun fighters of the classic westerns. Each wanted to be 'the fastest gun in the West', instantly ready to fire.

One major problem with the control of nuclear forces is that the "brains" would be the first target of attack. What happens if Washington D.C. and the US President are destroyed? What happens if the command and control systems are destroyed? When the top-level commanders are destroyed, lower-level commanders must take over; but then how will unauthorized firings be prevented?" *(1A-06)*

There is also a danger of the Nuclear Arsenal going into the wrong (terrorist) hands. But the responsibility for the future security of the world lies not just in preventing wrong hands from getting powerful, but also in preventing powerful hands from possible wrong action.

As Henry Kissinger once observed, *"The greatest danger of nuclear war lies not in the deliberate action of wicked men, but in the inability of harassed men to manage events that have run away from them. This surely describes the future."*

A few hundred nuclear warheads are enough to destroy the entire human civilization, and we have accumulated nearly twenty thousand of them on our planet.

There is no moral force acting against this; no outrage shown by the church or by any religious leaders against this massive accumulation.

THE ROLE OF PUGWASH IN THE RESOLUTION OF THE 1962 CUBAN MISSILE CRISIS

Nikita Khrushchev brought the world to the edge of the abyss by installing Soviet missiles with nuclear warheads in Cuba; in the most provocative and perilous trial of nuclear deterrence. Rotblat's response was to transmit a cable signed by American Pugwash scientists to their colleagues in Moscow, asking them to urge the Soviet government to reroute the ships approaching Cuba, which were thought to be carrying more weapons. For their part, the Americans would do their utmost to persuade the Kennedy administration from taking precipitate action. Over several days, Rotblat was in almost continuous telephonic communication with Washington and Moscow, trying to organise an emergency meeting of the US and Soviet senior scientists in London. The intensity of the near catastrophe spurred both leaders to new disarmament efforts in the face of strident internal opposition. (1A-07)

THE DOOMSDAY EMBLEMATIC CLOCK

As I mentioned earlier, in 1953 the Doomsday Emblematic Clock stood at 2 minutes to midnight.

From 1954 to 1960, it gradually increased to 7 minutes to midnight.

The close shave in 1962 during the Cuban Missile Crisis as described above, represented a '1 in 6' probability of a nuclear attack. In my view (as will be explained later in this chapter), this was equivalent to the clock momentarily positioned at 6 seconds to midnight.

In 1963, there was a partial test ban treaty between the US and the Soviet Union. Consequent to this Test Ban Treaty, the clock was shifted to 12 minutes to midnight.

Between 1963 and 1980 the clock moved as shown below:
1968 - 7 minutes to midnight
1969 - 10 minutes to midnight
1972 - 12 minutes to midnight
1974 - 9 minutes to midnight
1980 - 7 minutes to midnight

THE 1981 FIRST STRIKE SCENARIO

The international climate deteriorated significantly during the years 1980 and 1981. Although the Americans and Soviets signed SALT II (the Second Strategic Arms Limitation Treaty), it was dead on arrival in the US Senate for ratification, largely because of the Soviet invasion of Afghanistan in December 1979. Both superpowers increased deployment of new missile systems in Europe, and departed from the defensive posture of nuclear deterrence to declare nuclear war thinkable. Joseph Rotblat dismissed President Carter's notion of limited nuclear war as an "asinine excuse" for escalating the nuclear arms race and warned that the "thinkable" war would soon become an all-out holocaust. At the same meeting, another prominent Pugwashite, Patricia Lindop, delivered a stirring speech that was greeted with thunderous applause. In January 1981, the editors of the Bulletin of the Atomic Scientists, advanced the hands of the emblematic clock forward from seven minutes to four minutes before midnight. This took place in the light of deteriorating superpower relations - against a background of an annual global armament budget of $600 billion and the existence of sixty thousand nuclear warheads.

Writing in the same edition of the Bulletin, Rotblat concentrated on the increased sophistication and fantastic precision of modern weapons that threatened to bring an unanswerable first-strike option into play again. "The notion that one side can choose to wage a limited nuclear war is absolute nonsense," he wrote, explaining why any use of tactical nuclear weapons in Europe was bound to escalate. Attacks on military targets in cities in the war zone would inevitably lead to attacks on targets in the adversary's homeland, to be followed eventually by a massive exchange. "One side can start a war," he said, "but it takes two sides to keep it limited." He thought governments were trying systematically to condition the public to accept the possibility of limited nuclear war, partly through promoting civil defence again, as with the "protect and survive" campaign in the UK. *(1A-07)*

THE DOOMSDAY EMBLEMATIC CLOCK

1981   -   4 minutes to midnight.

The Soviet invasion of Afghanistan hardened the US nuclear posture. Before he left office, President Jimmy Carter, pulled the United States out from the Olympic Games in Moscow and considered ways in which the United States could win a nuclear war. The rhetoric only intensified with the election of Ronald Reagan as President. Reagan scrapped any talk of arms control and proposed that the best way to end the Cold War was for the United States to win it.

THE STRATEGIC DEFENCE INITIATIVE (SDI)

Ronald Reagan planned to design a defence system that would intercept and destroy strategic ballistic missiles before they reached American soil. In essence, it was more like an offensive system aimed at mopping up any Soviet missiles fired in retaliation, after an American first strike. Russians would doubtlessly consider such an anti-missile system as part of a first-strike weapon aimed at them. Mainstream American scientists and all the Pugwashites in the United States vehemently criticised the initiative.

SEPTEMBER 26 1983 - WORLD WAR 3 COULD HAVE STARTED.

"It is hard to imagine anything more devastating for humanity than an all-out nuclear war between Russia and the United States. Yet this might have occurred by accident on September 26, 1983; were it not for the wise decisions of Stanislav Yevgrafovich Petrov. For this, he deserves humanity's profound gratitude. Let us resolve to work together to realise a world free from fear of nuclear weapons, remembering the courageous judgement of Stanislav Petrov."
Ban Ki Moon (Former US Secretary General)

One of the closest calls occurred when Stanislav Petrov chose to ignore the Soviet early-warning detection system, which had erroneously indicated five incoming American nuclear missiles. With his decision to ignore algorithms and instead follow his gut instinct, Petrov helped prevent an all-out nuclear war between the US and Russia.

But Petrov maintained a humble outlook on the event by saying, "I was just doing my job." At the time when the alert came, there was high tension between the two superpowers, the US and USSR as a result of the heavy US military build-up in the early eighties and Ronald Reagan's strong anti-Soviet rhetoric. Just a few days before that, the Soviet Union had shot down a Korean plane killing all 300 passengers. This aspect had to be considered by Petrov when he received the alert about the five missiles. He had just a few minutes to decide whether to treat the satellite data as a false alarm or report an incoming attack. Petrov relied on his gut instinct and believed it was unlikely that the US should fire only five missiles. Accordingly, he informed his commanders that it was a false alarm.

It was later revealed that certain reflections of the sun and cloud tops had fooled the satellite into interpreting wrongly that it was detecting missile launchings. *(1A-07A)*

MIKHAIL GORBACHEV'S POSITIVE APPROACH IGNORED BY THE UNITED STATES

In January 1986, Mikhail Gorbachev prepared the text of a three-stage plan to eliminate all nuclear weapons from the face of the earth by the end of 1999. He sent a letter to Reagan with this three-stage plan. The response from Reagan was not forthcoming. He persisted in talking about the SDI development and did not join the Soviets in a nuclear test moratorium.

The same year in April, there was the devastating fire at the Chernobyl nuclear reactor. This served to reinforce Gorbachev's antinuclear sentiments. Two weeks after the catastrophe, during a televised speech, he pointed out that it "once again showed what an abyss will open up if nuclear war befalls mankind." The impact of the fire was considered equal to the German invasion of 1941. After Chernobyl, it was believed that "the nuclear danger ceased to be just something abstract; it became tangible and concrete." *(1A-07)*

The nuclear reactor accidents and radiation hazards became serious topics of discussion in the subsequent Pugwash conferences.

Gorbachev was always very serious about immediate deep cuts in the arsenals of both superpowers. In the aftermath of Chernobyl, Moscow was "so scared of 'accidental' war, that a special unit was formed under the Chief-of-Staff of machinery, to deal with the problem on a continuous basis."

In December 1988, Mikhail Gorbachev gave a speech of historical significance at the United Nations in New York.

It seemed to lift the Iron Curtain, whose descent Churchill described so memorably four decades ago. While he may have lacked Churchill's grandiloquence, the content of Gorbachev's speech was detailed and bold. He announced the unilateral shrinkage of Soviet armed forces by five hundred thousand men, with commensurate reductions in conventional armaments within two years. He also spoke about the withdrawal of six tank divisions from Eastern European states, within three years. He explained that these and other fallbacks of clearly defensive positions were in line with the new "principle of reasonable defence sufficiency." *(1A-07)*

Once again, the response from the United States was not at all forthcoming. George H.W.Bush did not grasp the epoch-ending status of Gorbachev's speech nor the final departure of the Soviet troops from Afghanistan in February 1989. Gorbachev, still intent on nuclear disarmament, wanted to eliminate all short-range tactical nuclear weapons from Europe, and announced the unilateral withdrawal of five hundred warheads in May that year. Still, there was no response from the United States, except to remark that Gorbachev "was throwing out arms control proposals like a drugstore cowboy." However, George H.W.Bush's administration did enter negotiations that would culminate in the Conventional Armed Forces Treaty (CFE), within a short span of two years.

THE NOBEL PEACE PRIZE

Rotblat and the Pugwash conferences shared the Nobel Peace Prize in 1995. Rotblat delivered his acceptance speech titled "Remember Your Humanity," and was rewarded with a standing ovation. Following the award, Rotblat became a public figure. He was lauded as the conscience of nuclear science, and was invited to lectures all over the world. In his Nobel lecture, Rotblat placed customary emphasis on the social responsibility of scientists, suggesting that whistleblowing should also become a part of a scientist's ethos. *(1A-05)*

SWIMMING AGAINST THE CURRENT: RESPONSIBLE DISSIDENCE

Mordechai Vanunu, served an eighteen-year sentence in solitary confinement for revealing details to the London Sunday Times about the manufacture of plutonium at the Dimona Nuclear Plant in Israel, where he had worked as a technician. His disclosures could not be refuted by the Israeli government and exposed a large hole in their policy of nuclear opacity. Rotblat played a predominant role in the campaign to free Vanunu. He hosted a seminar entitled "Swimming against the Current: Responsible Dissidence," taking Sakharov as his exemplar. He credited Sakharov with exposing the hypocrisy of the Soviet Union over nuclear disarmament during the Cold War. Rotblat considered Vanunu's act as a generational act for the world, not a malicious attempt to harm Israel. *(1A-05)*

ROTBLAT'S TEN-POINT MEMO

At a meeting in New York, Rotblat presented a memo on the rationale, prerequisites and implementation of a nuclear weapon free world (NWFW) *(1A-07)*.

It contained ten essential points:
* Nuclear disarmament is a legal obligation under Article 6 of the NPT.
* Reduction of a few hundred weapons is not acceptable as it is unstable and will not stick. The only way to stabilise the situation is to ensure zero nuclear weapons.
* The most succinct reason for elimination is McNamara's. He states: "The indefinite combination of human fallibility and nuclear weapons, carries a high risk of a potential catastrophe."
* The Nuclear Weapons Convention (NWC), should be based on the Chemical Weapons Convention, and make possession of the same a crime under International Law.
* The NWC should be universal, and once ratified by a certain number of states, it should become mandatory for all others. There should be no provision for withdrawal whatsoever.
* All secret research should be outlawed.
* There should be a clause mandating all the states to pass national laws and calling on citizens to notify an international authority in case of an attempt to violate the convention.
* This will only come about, if the five Nuclear Weapon States (NWS), agree that this is in their best interest. It will be unlikely that they would then violate the NWC, by retaining any nuclear weapons.
* Attempts to violate the NWC by a rogue state, can and will be dealt with by conventional military force only. Any decision about enforcement would be taken by the UN Security Council.
* There should be an international authority to monitor progress of dismantlement and implementation. All sites where weapons-useable fissile material exists - whether civilian or military - should be internationally supervised and guarded.

THE DOOMSDAY EMBLEMATIC CLOCK

Between 1984 and 1999 the clock moved as follows:
1984 - 3 minutes to midnight
1988 - 6 minutes to midnight
1990 - 10 minutes to midnight
1991 - 17 minutes to midnight
1995 - 14 minutes to midnight
1998 - 9 minutes to midnight

THE WORLD OTHER THAN A COLD WAR WORLD

Notwithstanding the enormous contribution of Pugwash in reducing the Cold War conflicts, the geopolitics of the world other than the United States/Soviet world, have remained largely unaffected by the Pugwash movement. Leaders of nations in general are largely unaware of the Pugwash conferences or may be indifferent to them.

THE KARGIL WAR OF 1999

Indian Prime Minister Atal Bihari Vajpayee, visited Lahore, Pakistan in early 1999. It was a historic visit; seen by the people of the two countries as a significant move towards establishment of peace between them. I distinctly remember a 'feel good factor' generated by Vajpayee's visit. But it was not to be.

Pakistan shattered the peace process. About 700 men from the 10th Corps of Pakistan's army crossed the line of control and infiltrated into Indian territory. Full-fledged war between India and Pakistan was the obvious outcome. The Indian response was executed bearing in mind the limitations of fighting a war under a nuclear overhang. The US condemned Pakistan's infiltration of armed intruders, saw Pakistan as the aggressor, and rejected the fiction that the fighters were separatist guerrillas. The Clinton administration made it clear that if Nawaz Sharif (the Pakistan Prime Minister at the time), did not order a pullback, it would hold up a

$100 million International Monetary Fund loan that Pakistan sorely needed.

Here is an extract from an article written by Strobe Talbot, a member of Clinton's team of advisers *(1A-08)*:

"On Friday, July 2, Sharif phoned Clinton and pleaded for his personal intervention in South Asia. Clinton replied that he would consider it only if it was understood up-front that Pakistani withdrawal would have to be immediate and unconditional.

The next day, Sharif called Clinton to say that he was packing his bags and getting ready to fly immediately to Washington - never mind that he had not been invited. He warned Sharif not to come unless he was prepared to announce unconditional withdrawal; otherwise his trip would make a bad situation worse. The Pakistani leader did not accept Clinton's condition for the meeting - he just said he was on his way.

"This guy's coming literally on a wing and a prayer," said the President.

"That's right," said Bruce Riedel [NSC aide]. "And he is praying that we don't make him do the one thing he has got to do to end this thing."

It was not hard to anticipate what Sharif would ask for. His opening proposal would be a cease-fire to be followed by negotiation under American auspices. His fallback would make Pakistani withdrawal conditional on India's agreement to direct negotiations sponsored and probably mediated by the United States. Either way, he would be able to claim that the incursion had forced India - under American pressure - to accept Pakistani terms.

After several long meetings in Sandy Berger's office, we decided to recommend that Clinton confront Sharif with a stark choice that included neither of his preferred options. We would put before him two press statements, and let Sharif decide which would be released at the end of the Blair House talks. The first would hail him as a peacemaker for retreating - or as we would put it euphemistically, 'restoring and respecting the sanctity of the Line of Control.' The second would blame him for starting the crisis and for the escalation, sure to follow his failed mission to Washington.

On the eve of Sharif's arrival, we learned that Pakistan might be preparing its nuclear forces for deployment. There was among those of us preparing for the meeting, a sense of vast and nearly unprecedented peril. When Clinton assembled his advisers in the Oval Office for a last-minute huddle, Sandy told him that overnight, we had gotten more disturbing reports of the steps Pakistan was taking with its nuclear arsenal. Clinton said he would like to use this information 'to scare the hell out of Sharif.'

Sandy told the President that he was heading into what would probably be the single, most important meeting with a foreign leader of his entire presidency. It would also be one of the most delicate. The overriding objective was to induce Pakistani withdrawal. But another, probably incompatible goal was to increase the chances of Sharif's political survival. "If he arrives as a prime minister but stays as an exile," said Sandy, "he is not going to be able to stick to whatever deal you get out of him." We had to find a way to provide Sharif just enough cover to go home and give the necessary orders to Musharraf and the military.

The conversation had already convinced Clinton of what he feared: the world was even closer to a nuclear war, than during the Cuban Missile Crisis. Unlike Kennedy and Khrushchev in 1962, Vajpayee and Sharif did not realise how close they were to the brink, so there was an even greater risk that they would blindly stumble across it.

Adding to the danger was evidence that Sharif neither knew everything his military high command was doing nor had complete control over it. When Clinton asked him if he understood how far along his military was in preparing nuclear-armed missiles for possible use in a war against India, Sharif acted as though he was genuinely surprised. He said he could believe that the Indians were taking such steps, but he neither acknowledged nor seemed aware of anything like that on his own side.

Clinton decided to invoke the Cuban Missile Crisis; noting that it had been a formative experience for him (he had been sixteen at the time). Now, India and Pakistan were similarly on the edge of a precipice. If even one bomb was used (Sharif finished the sentence), "it would be a catastrophe."

He [Clinton] returned to the offensive. He could see they were getting nowhere. Fearing that might be the result, he had a statement ready to release to the press in time for the evening news show that would lay all the blame for the crisis on Pakistan. Sharif went ashen.

Clinton bore down harder. Having listened to Sharif's complaints against the United States, he had a list of his own, and it started with terrorism. Pakistan was the principal sponsor of the Taliban, which in turn allowed Osama Bin Laden to run his worldwide network out of Afghanistan. Clinton had asked Sharif repeatedly to cooperate in bringing Bin Laden to justice. Sharif had promised to do so but failed to deliver. The statement the United States would make to the press would mention Pakistan's role in supporting terrorism in Afghanistan, and through its backing of Kashmiri militants, in India as well. Was that what Sharif wanted?

Clinton had worked himself back into real anger - his face flushed, eyes narrowed, lips pursed, cheek muscles pulsing, fists clenched. He said it was crazy enough for Sharif to have let his military violate the Line of Control, start a border war with India, and now prepare nuclear forces for action. On top of that, he had put Clinton in the middle of the mess and set him up for a diplomatic failure.

Sharif seemed beaten, physically and emotionally. He denied he had given any orders regarding nuclear weaponry, and said he was worried for his own life.

When the two leaders had been at it for an hour and a half, Clinton suggested a break so that both could consult with their teams. The President and Riedel briefed Sandy, Rick, and me on what had happened. Now that he had made maximum use of the "bad statement" we had prepared in advance, Clinton said it was time to deploy the good one.

Clinton took a catnap on a sofa in a small study off the main entryway while Bruce, Sandy, Rick, and I cobbled together a new version of the "good statement," incorporating some of the Pakistani language from the paper that Sharif had claimed was in play between him and Vajpayee. But the key sentence in the new document was ours, not his, and it would nail the one thing we had to get out of the talks: 'The Prime Minister has agreed to take concrete and immediate steps for the restoration of the Line of Control.' The paper called for a ceasefire but only after the Pakistanis went back on their side of the line. It reaffirmed Clinton's longstanding plan to visit South Asia.

The meeting came quickly to a happy and friendly end, at least on Clinton's part." *(1A-08)*

THE DOOMSDAY EMBLEMATIC CLOCK

The close shave in the 1999 Kargil War, as described above, represented a 1 in 5 probability of a nuclear attack. In my view (as explained later) this was equivalent to the needle of the emblematic clock momentarily positioned at 5 seconds to midnight.

M. S. SWAMINATHAN'S MESSAGE

In January 2003, a symposium called "Science and Beyond" was held in Bangalore. Professor M. S. Swaminathan, who was the president of the Pugwash movement at the time, delivered a sterling message in his talk, "Science, Peace, and Sustainable Development" as follows:

"Scientists and technologists have a particularly vital role to play in launching an ethical revolution. The Pugwash movement, which I now have the privilege to lead, is an expression of the social and moral duty of scientists, to promote the beneficial applications of their work, prevent their misuse, to anticipate and evaluate the possible unintended consequences of scientific and technological development, and to promote debate and reflection of the 'ethical obligations of scientists in taking responsibility for their work.' It will be appropriate to quote, in this context, what Bertrand Russell and Albert Einstein said, in their famous manifesto of 1955, issued on the occasion of the tenth anniversary of the use of atom bombs on Hiroshima and Nagasaki:

'We appeal as human beings to human beings. Remember your humanity and forget the rest. If you can do so, the way lies open to a new paradise; if you cannot, there lies before you the risk of universal death.'

Shall we renounce war and violence as a method of settling disputes, or shall we put an end to the human civilization? This is the question facing us today. We are witnessing a growing intolerance of diversity and pluralism in human societies; for example, in terms of religion, ethnicity, political belief, colour, culture, gender, and language. The confluence of science and religion should be reflected in all areas of human inquiry. The growing violence in the human heart that we witness today, underlines the urgency of ensuring that science and technology are employed for human happiness and not its destruction. The Pugwash movement has been constantly reminding scientists of their ethical responsibility for the consequences of their research, and governments of the immorality, illegality and peril inherent in nuclear weapons." (1A-09)

CHARLES TOWNES'S VIEW ON SCIENCE AND RELIGION

In the same seminar, the great scientist and philosopher Charles Townes gave the following message:

"There are two fundamental reasons why I believe that religion and science must be parallel and must interact. One is that if there is purpose and meaning in the universe, then the purpose must be related to its structure, and in fact must determine its structure. The second is that in both fields, we use all our human abilities in a quest to understand the world we inhabit. Religion and science are more similar in terms of our efforts to understand than we normally think. Among the public, it is very common to believe that scientists simply design their experiments, write their equations, use logic, and then conclude - objectively and without questioning what the truth is. And that is it. Religion on the other hand, is often viewed as a matter of faith alone. In this view, religion is about things we do not know and cannot prove, things that belong to the domain of the emotions. In fact, we use all our human abilities in both endeavors. In both realms, we want to understand. The Nobel Laureate scientist, Bridgman of Harvard University, who was also known as something of a philosopher, was once asked to define the scientific method. Bridgman said, 'The scientific method? That is to work like the devil to find the answer, with no holds barred.' Well, that is just what it is. We use our every instinct, our every ability, to do the best science that we are capable of. I deeply believe that the same is true in religion. The emphasis may be different, but the striving to understand is similar. And this striving to understand, using all our abilities, represents a broad parallel between these two great activities of the human spirit." (1A-09)

CURRENT GEOPOLITICS OF THE WORLD

The subject must be understood from a neutral perspective. The task here is to analyse all the 'Information in the Field', and to understand what happened in the past - how it happened, what is happening now, and what can happen in the future.

AMERICAN INTERFERENCES

America was once considered the best place in the world to be in.

In the words of Einstein, *"It has an international 'psyche.' It constitutes the bulwark of the democratic way of life, it has demonstrated that individual freedom provides a better basis for productive labour than any form of tyranny, and its political and economic position is so powerful that it can help the world by breaking the tradition of war from which the world suffered." (1A-10)*

All that has changed. Having become rich and powerful, America also tended to become selfish and arrogant. Selfish, because it started grabbing a disproportionately higher share of the world's resources, and arrogant because in order to ensure the safety and security of its own people, America began to undertake large-scale interference in the affairs of other countries. This interference was manipulated to create rifts between nations, or between two segments of the same nation with which America interfered. To add insult to injury, America turned a blind eye to these rifts.

American interference in the Middle East - where they prefer dictatorships to secular liberal democracies (so that it is easy for dictators to align with common causes and grab the resources of a country) - is responsible for disenchantment of the common people in these countries and consequent unrest. It is an established fact that the United States, with the help of Israel, did not allow secular nationalism to prevail in many countries in the Middle East. Rather, they destroyed secular nationalism, and this created Islamic fundamentalist extremism.

It would not be out of place to provide here an extract from Noam Chomsky's book *"What We Say Goes"*:

"Since the second world war, the United States has been the world's strongest outside supporter of extremist Islamist fundamentalism. Washington's oldest and most valued ally in the Arab World is Saudi

Arabia. Iran looks like a democratic heaven in comparison. The threat to Saudi Arabian religious extremist tyranny was secular nationalism, mainly embodied by Gamal Abdel Nasser. So, Nasser became an enemy, because he threatened the US base of extremist religious fundamentalism - Saudi Arabia, which happens to control the oil, the underlying reason. In 1967, Israel performed a huge service to the United States, to Saudi Arabia, and the energy corporations, by essentially eliminating secular Arab nationalism, which was threatening to use the resources of the region for the needs of its own population.

The same thing has happened time after time. Israel created Hamas by destroying the secular Palestine Liberation Organization, which was calling for negotiations and settlement. Since that was the last thing the United States and Israel wanted, they destroyed it. And then what happened? The population didn't disintegrate; they turned to something else - in this case, religious fundamentalism.

In Pakistan, the movement relating to radical Islamism began with former President Muhammad Zia-ul-Haq, who was strongly supported by the Reagan administration. In fact, all through its tenure, the Reagan administration pretended that Zia wasn't developing nuclear weapons. Of course, they knew that he was. But, every year, they would religiously certify that Pakistan was not developing nuclear weapons, because they wanted to support their radical extremist fundamentalist friend. They knew perfectly well that Saudi Arabia was funding the extremist madrassas - the religious schools that undermined the Pakistani educational system, which had been pretty good beforehand. You could not get students to study sciences, because schools teach only the Koran. That wasn't true in the past. The Reagan administration supported all these developments." *(1A-11)*

The 9/11 Terrorist attack on the World Trade Centre was a consequence of American Interferences in the Middle East.

THE BUSH INVASION OF IRAQ IN 2003 AND ITS CONSEQUENCES

By far the single most act of blundering error of judgment (or stupidity) was George W. Bush's invasion of Iraq in 2003. This resulted in the death of more than two hundred thousand civilians, and the recent civil wars in Iraq and Syria.

Consider this passage by Rotblat:

"Neither of the three reasons presented for the launch of the attacks – namely to eliminate Saddam's weapons of mass destruction, to destroy the link with Al-Qaeda, and to overthrow a bad regime - were acceptable to the world. The main reason was that the United States was pursuing global dominance intermittently since the Second World War. From the very beginning, the development of nuclear weapons was used by the United States, to give them a dominant position in the world. At the beginning, they were determined not to allow any other nation to have nuclear weapons."

Rotblat believed that President Bush's disregard for arms control treaties, coupled with an interest in developing new nuclear warheads, threatened the progress that had been made in nuclear disarmament over the past two decades. Regarding morality and equity in world affairs, Rotblat stated the following:

"It is the United States that has to be called to order. It is intolerable that in this day and age, the mightiest country in the world should have declared that its overriding motivation in international affairs was the self-interest of the United States of America. I cannot help the feeling that selfishness and greed - which became the driving force after the victory of capitalism in the ideological struggle - are to some extent responsible for the terrible carnage that we have just witnessed." (1A-07)

That the recent civil wars in Iraq and Syria, were also a consequence of American interference is not difficult to understand.

The invasion resulted in tens of thousands of civilian casualties. Friends and relatives of those killed in the Sunni faction became terrorists; so it became a justification to fight them. A government and a local army were installed to fight remnant terrorism. This army was predominantly made up of another faction, Shias, but it had several Sunnis, too. At the behest of the Bush government, the Sunnis were thrown out of the Iraqi Army. They had no jobs and nowhere to go. They became victims of time, caused by the interactions of the world. When the American forces withdrew from Iraq - which turned out to be a great error of judgment by Barack Obama - those who were in possession of weapons became terrorists. Others of their faction acquired weapons and joined them; they did not join them as fighters but simply supported them. They took in their control large areas of Iraq as well as Syria. They are called ISIS. There is nothing religious about them or their actions. As explained earlier, they are all made up of disgruntled people, insecure and unhappy victims of time, caused by the interactions of the world. They picked up discontent young people from all over the world - mostly Europe; sympathised with them and enticed them to join. If the essence of religion, any religion, is to "live and let live" in peace and harmony, then there is nothing religious in what they do. They take advantage of the contradictions in their religious document, which according to their own interpretations permits them to indulge in jihad against Non-Muslims. If they die, they are promised a place in heaven by their leaders. It is a natural selection virus called "to live and let die" that enters their minds which causes conflicts and wars. It has infected the minds of the leaders, and they are injecting the virus into the minds and bodies of normal, innocent human beings in a way, so as to create a different kind of virus called "to die and let die".

LIMITS ON WAR

Given below is an extract from V. R. Raghavan's review of the book India's Sentinel. It is about Air Commodore Jasjit Singh's select writings on the subject:

"On nuclear deterrence, Jasjit was a pioneer in highlighting the limits nuclear weapons placed on fighting wars. He was emphatic that the 'sheer existence of nuclear weapons with both adversaries, imposes major limitations on the way force and violence can be used against each other without risking a nuclear exchange. This alters the very nature of war.' This axiom was soon proved in Kargil, when Pakistan used its army to occupy the heights on and across the LOC. This had led to an Indian response that was executed bearing in mind Jasjit's warning on the nuclear weapons. This in turn led to a wide-ranging debate on fighting a 'limited war' under a nuclear overhang. While the debate is yet inconclusive, it nevertheless proves the merit of the argument that nuclear weapons have indeed changed the way war will be fought by two nuclear adversaries." *(1A-12)*

Military force is no longer the answer. Conflict through terrorism is considered more effective by the Pakistan Army, not to mention substantially cheaper. The extract continues:

"The Pakistan Army believes terror is an instrument of state policy, for which, as Jasjit Singh's writings show, military force is not the answer. The belief that Pakistan can be weaned from this strategy by concessions through appeasement talks, is seen by many as a misplaced notion. Pakistan has changed rapidly in the last decade and is currently in a state of political and economic uncertainty." *(1A-12)*

THE DOOMSDAY EMBLEMATIC CLOCK

This is how the clock moved between 2002 and 2015

2002 - 7 minutes to midnight
2007 - 5 minutes to midnight
2010 - 6 minutes to midnight
2012 - 5 minutes to midnight

HIGHLY SIGNIFICANT "INFORMATION IN THE FIELD" FROM CALIFORNIA IN NOVEMBER 2015 - BRIGHT LIGHT IN THE SKY:

What then was the real purpose behind the nuclear test carried out by the US Navy in November 2015 in California?

A friend (in fact my brother-in-law, Dr. A.P.Hannda) who had been reading my manuscript 'Information in the Field', came across a blog on **investmentwatchblog.com**. He promptly emailed it to me thinking it might interest me to include some of that information in my section on 'IITF'.

The blog was by Mike Adams. The following is an excerpt from his Natural News blog on **investmentwatchblog.com** - *"Thermonuclear Missile Launch near Los Angeles Is the Final Sign of World War III on the Precipice; US, China, and Russia All Escalating Covert Attacks in Run-Up to Global War." (1A-13)*

"Media in California confirmed that the light came from an unarmed Trident missile fired from the USS Kentucky navy submarine, reports the BBC. While they call the missile 'unarmed,' they fail to mention that the Trident missile normally carries a thermonuclear warhead. There is also no way for the media to know whether this missile was really unarmed or not, as the sole source on that is the US Navy itself.

Obviously, the official cover story is pure bunk. So, what is the real story behind this? It all has to do with China and the covert war that is already underway between China, the United States and Russia. Ronald O'Rourke, Specialist in Naval Affairs, had earlier on September 21, 2015 released a report titled - 'China Navel Modernisation: Implications for US Naval capabilities.'

The report states:

China is building a modern and regionally powerful navy with a limited but growing capability for conducting operations beyond China's near-seas region. Observers of Chinese and US military forces, view China's improving naval capabilities as posing a potential challenge in the Western Pacific to the US Navy's ability to achieve and maintain control of blue-water ocean areas in wartime - the first such challenge the US Navy has faced since the end of the Cold War.

China's naval modernisation effort encompasses a broad array of platform and weapon acquisition programs, including Anti-Ship Ballistic Missiles (ASBMs), Anti-Ship Cruise Missiles (ASCMs), submarines, surface ships, aircrafts and supporting C4ISR (command and control, communications, computers, intelligence, surveillance, and reconnaissance) systems.

The most important section of this report is this description of China's ship-killing ballistic missiles:

China is fielding an ASBM, referred to as the DF-21D, which is a theatre-range ballistic missile equipped with a maneuverable re-entry vehicle (MaRV), designed to hit moving ships at sea. DOD states that China continues to field an ASBM, based on a variant of the CSS-5 (DF-21) MR.BM that it began deploying in 2010. This missile provides the PLA, the capability to attack aircraft carriers in the Western Pacific. The CSS-5 Mod 5, has a range exceeding 1,500 km [about 810 nm] and is armed with a maneuverable warhead.

China, in other words, has weapons capable of destroying US aircraft carriers, destroyers, and other ships. The 1,500-kilometer range is key as it allows a very wide operational range.

Recently, in August 2015, the Chinese and Russians held their largest naval joint exercise in history as a way to counter US influence in Asia.

The following was reported by www.collapse.news:

'The Russian and Chinese navies are set to hold their largest joint exercises ever, featuring scores of warships, hundreds of troops, and an amphibious landing, in what appears to be a deepening of ties meant to counter a rising US military presence in Asia.'

In September 2015, Chinese warships were spotted operating near the coast of Alaska. This was reported across the mainstream media, including the **Wall Street Journal**, in an article titled 'Five Chinese Navy Ships Are Operating in Bering Sea off Alaska.'

Fox News also covered the same story, 'Five Chinese Warships Spotted Off Alaska Coast' during President Obama's Visit.

In response to that territorial provocation, the US Navy sent the USS Lassen destroyer within twelve nautical miles of China's newly-constructed military bases in the Spratly Islands. China's communist government openly condemned the act as a provocation of war.

Following is an excerpt from the Straits Times:

'China claims most of the South China Sea, and on October 9, its foreign ministry warned that Beijing would never allow any country to violate China's territorial waters and airspace in the Spratly Islands, in the name of protecting freedom of navigation and overflight.'

What then was the purpose behind the US Navy's 'showcasing' of the Trident missile near Los Angeles in November 2015?

The simple answer: It was a $31 million billboard that told China: ***"DON'T MEDDLE WITH US!"***

Mike Adams continues: "Nobody in the mainstream media is reporting this, probably because with a few exceptions, they are mostly clueless, brain-dead propagandists who know nothing about international geopolitics and the real state of conflict in our world. Also, they are ordered what to write by the US government regime in exactly the same way China's 'journalists' are ordered what to write by the Chinese regime.

Right now, the United States and China are in an undeclared state of war. China stands ready to strike the United States with nuclear warheads or high altitude EMP weapons that would destroy the US power grid, and cause casualties in the range of 90 percent across the unprepared population.

Many people believe that China and Russia are working together to prepare for a massive first strike against the United States that would cripple its defenses and economy. Following that first strike, a land invasion would commence, using Russian troops.

Supporting this theory, Russian submarines have been spotted near undersea internet cables, in an obvious effort to document their whereabouts so that the cables can be instantly severed, unleashing a devastating blow to the US economy including Wall Street, and even military communications.

'Russian submarines and spy ships are aggressively operating near the vital undersea cables that carry almost all global internet communications, raising concerns among some American military and intelligence officials that the Russians might be planning to attack those lines in times of conflict,' reports WND.com. 'In times of tension or conflict, the ultimate Russian hack on the United States could involve severing the fiber-optic cables at some of their hardest-to-access locations, in order to halt the instant communications on which the West's governments, economies, and citizens have grown dependent.'

At the same time, a new Russian 'drone sub' has been created that can strike the US coastal cities and harbours with nuclear weapons.

If you put the pieces of this puzzle together, what is really shaping up here is a massive, multi-layered pre-emptive strike against America, an empire seen by the rest of the world as an insane bully that meddles with everything on the international stage. This first strike, combining the forces and expertise of both China and Russia, may consist of the following:

1. *High-altitude EMP detonation over North America, destroying regional power grids.*
2. *A devastating currency war initiated by China, announcing its own gold-backed currency while dumping the US Treasury debt on the open market.*
3. *A Russian led severing of undersea fiber-optic cables.*
4. *Russian launched nuclear missiles targeting the US coastal cities.*
5. *A China led assault on the US Navy warships using anti-ship ballistic missiles (ASBMs).*
6. *A cyber warfare attack on key US infrastructures, including water delivery systems, nuclear power plants and the power grid.*

While all this was being predicted, the Obama administration was busy firing all the top military commanders who knew how to survive such an assault.

The Congress has now heard testimony that the United States is not ready for World War III while Russia is chomping at the bit to 'get it on.' Further, the Congress has learned that Obama has once again been badly outmaneuvered by Putin, the master chess player. The Chinese and the Russians are going to kick America's rear end in the upcoming war." (1A-13)

THE DOOMSDAY EMBLEMATIC CLOCK

In the year 2015, the needle of the Doomsday Emblematic Clock was shifted to 3 minutes to midnight.

STATUS AS ON DECEMBER 2016

Donald Trump won the US election in November 2016. He considers Putin a great friend. Trump and Putin have been mutually admiring and continuously praising each other for quite some time. Following Trump's election, Putin found no difficulty in helping Assad and the Syrian government forces close in and finally retake Aleppo from the rebels. But the civil war in Syria is far from over. As long as the Sunnis are in majority in Syria, they will not like to be ruled by a Shia led government; the unrest may continue, unless and until the two factions unite.

The big news of the last few days is that the CIA has found out about Russia's role in successfully manipulating the US elections to ensure that Trump gets elected. Obama is furious, has called for an investigation. Some people consider this interference by Russia extremely serious; of the same magnitude as the Pearl Harbor attack or the 9/11 attack.

Another big news of the last few days is that Trump has offended China big time by warming up to the Taiwan President.

Yet another big news is that Trump may not support Iran's Nuclear Deal with the US and other countries. This may infuriate Iran.

The equation is now extremely complex. Putin's capacity as a 'master chess player' to manipulate and outmaneuver, along with Trump's lack of knowledge and understanding about what is going on in the world, does not - at this stage - auger well for world peace.

Donald Trump during his election campaign spelt out his intent in bringing about some changes that according to him could make America great again. However, the same changes according to the general world opinion could endanger world peace, including the peace in America.

The big news as the year 2016 ended was that the UN has passed a resolution for a Two State solution of the Israel- Palestine issue. The resolution was passed with 14 votes in favour and none against. US abstained and did not veto this. The US Secretary of State John Kerry, delivered a stunning speech on 28th December 2016 that lasted for seventy minutes.

Kerry strongly defended the US decision to allow a UN resolution, condemning Israeli settlements, saying if Washington had vetoed it, Israel would have been given a license for 'unfettered settlement construction,' and that would be the end of the peace process.

Israeli Prime Minister, Benjamin Netanyahu, strongly criticised the resolution as well as the Obama Administration. He made his intentions clear by stating that he will not abide by the resolution. Donald Trump also criticised the resolution and is supporting Netanyahu. He told him not to worry and that 20th January 2017 (the date fixed for his taking over as President) is fast approaching.

What exactly Trump is going to do depends on his interactions with the world. As I mentioned, the equation is now extremely complex, and it is quite difficult to predict what may happen in the coming years.

THE DOOMSDAY EMBLEMATIC CLOCK

In the first week of January 2017, while the editing of 'Intelligent Field' was in process, I added a two-page section on 'Current Status - December 2016,' in the chapter 'Information in The Field'. The following lines were a part of this section:

"My guess is that the needle of the emblematic clock might have just moved closer to midnight by at least half a minute, the day Trump was elected President. I hope I am wrong."

Later that month, the following headlines appeared in the Bangalore edition of the Times of India:

"The Doomsday Emblematic Clock moved 30 seconds closer to midnight."

In April 2017, the clock stood at two and a half minutes to midnight.

ABOUT ICAN, NBT AND DR. TILMAN RUFF

"The International Campaign to Abolish Nuclear Weapons (ICAN), was awarded the Nobel Peace Prize in 2017, for 'its work to draw attention to the catastrophic humanitarian consequences of any use of nuclear weapons, and for its ground-breaking efforts to achieve a treaty-based prohibition of such weapons' - The Norwegian Nobel Committee.

Dr. Tilman Ruff is the founder of ICAN; a coalition of nongovernmental organizations in one hundred countries, promoting adherence to and implementation of the United Nations Nuclear Weapon Ban Treaty (NBT), which was adopted in New York on 7 July 2017.

Dr. Ruff drew specific attention to the need for disarmament education so that the public is genuinely aware not only of the current threat posed by nuclear weapons, but also of the role of their own government's policy in either consolidating the current nuclear architecture or its efforts to abolish it. In dismantling the current nuclear architecture, civil society can draw from the ample scientific evidence against nuclear weapons; there simply is no protection from the effects of the use of nuclear weapons. The effects of nuclear war will affect humans and the environment alike. Even smaller nuclear weapon arsenals of France, China, UK, India, Israel and Pakistan, pose a global threat, since their eventual use will affect human, animal and plant lives, along with the climate and agriculture alike. This reality of nuclear weapons prompts Dr. Ruff to liken present existing defence doctrines relying on nuclear weapons to a doctrine of self-assured destruction, and nuclear weapons pose an existential threat to humanity at large.

Regardless of abundant scientific data against nuclear weapons, Dr. Ruff pointed out that it was only 68 years after the bombings of Hiroshima and Nagasaki (in 1945), that governments agreed to discuss the humanitarian impact of nuclear weapons. Three massive humanitarian conferences were convened to discuss the matter in Oslo, Norway (2013), Nayarit, Mexico (2014) and Vienna, Austria (2014). The evidence against nuclear weapons was understood by the governments participating in these conferences. However, not all states (especially nuclear weapon states), took part. Dr. Ruff also pointed out that, till date, no government has commissioned a study on the climate and agricultural impact of nuclear weapons.

NUCLEAR FREE WORLD OR NUCLEAR WEAPON WORLD?

Nuclear armed states, especially the United States, have exercised considerable pressure on other states not to sign the NBT. Sweden is a case in point: the US Defence Secretary Mattis, directly threatened Sweden not to sign the NBT, or else Sweden's defence co-operation and eventual NATO membership would be at risk. It appears that nuclear armed states are indeed worried about the NBT, and this in itself is a sign that the NBT matters.

As pointed out by Dr. Ruff, humanity is currently at crossroads. One lane leads to a nuclear free world with the NBT being one of the tools in achieving this purpose. The other lane is a world in which the states continue to possess nuclear weapons. There is only one problem with the latter scenario: if the states continue to possess nuclear arsenals, nuclear weapons will be used sooner or later. Dr. Ruff draws attention to serious tensions between NATO and Russia, US and China, and in several parts of the world, such as Ukraine, Middle East and South East Asia.

At the same time, nuclear threats and the intention to use these weapons, is openly affirmed not only by the US and Russia, but also by others such as UK, India and Pakistan. The continued existence of nuclear weapons is strengthened by the significant underlying arms industry and the enormous governmental investments therein; the global annual expenditure on nuclear weapons is estimated at US $105 billion or $12 million an hour. Dr. Ruff concludes that there is currently no commitment to nuclear disarmament evident among the nuclear armed states and their accomplices.

Dr. Ruff acknowledged that the Pugwash Conferences on Science and World Affairs, have been doing significant and valuable work - often behind the scenes - in building dialogue on disarmament and non-proliferation, and in disarmament education. He also expressed his highest regard for one of the Pugwash founders, Prof. Joseph Rotblat."

(From the ICAN website)

THE SITUATION IN NORTH EAST ASIA

We start with an extract from an article by Pugwash:

"The dangers related to North Korean nuclear activities are very serious in terms of possible use of nuclear weapons. Even if the use of nuclear weapons by North Koreans would most likely imply the destruction of their country, the possibility of such use cannot be ruled out, as the North Korean leader may at some point even decide to 'sacrifice' the country for the 'cause.' Remember that in 1992 (30 years after the Cuban Missile Crisis), Robert McNamara while talking with Castro, learned that the Cuban President was ready to accept the destruction of the island if the US-USSR crisis was unable to be defused. There is in any case also a significant dimension related to proliferation in North East Asia. President Trump has suggested the possibility of re-deploying US nuclear weapons on South Korean territory. Moreover, even before becoming President, he had suggested that South Korea (and Japan), faced with the North Korean threat, should consider building their own nuclear weapons. Recent opinion polls suggest that in South Korea, 60% of the population may support building nuclear weapons as a defence against the North Korean nuclear threat, and

70% of the population even support the reintroduction of US nuclear weapons into South Korean territory. Faced with the possible spread of nuclear weapons on the Korean peninsula, Japan itself may very well consider the nuclear option. A general argument could be made here; if we were to witness the use of nuclear weapons against cities or military targets ever again, then the global non-proliferation regime would be shaken to its core."

DONALD TRUMP'S PROVOCATIVE APPROACH

Donald Trump came out with a barrage of extremely provocative statements against North Korea. Apart from signalling his intent in a United Nations meeting, he also indicated that he wants to destroy North Korea totally. A few examples are below:

- *'North Korea best not make any more threats to the United States. They will be met with fire and fury like the world has never seen. Kim Jong-un has been very threatening, beyond a normal statement. And as I said, they will be met with fire, fury, and frankly, power, the likes of which this world has never seen before.'*
- *'The era of strategic patience with the North Korean Regime has failed. Many years and its failed, and frankly that patience is over.'*

The above are just a couple of inflammatory comments made by Trump. There are many, many more.

Trump's reckless and extremely dangerous approach, emboldened Kim still further and placed South Korea in a deep fix. Trump made it clear that he cares only about America's interests. To continue kowtowing to Washington would be dangerous, even if Seoul cannot totally quit the pretence of honouring its long time ally - at least not yet. Indeed, the Trump presidency, less than a year old, had been a headache for President Moon, who won the elections in May, promising greater engagement and an end to hostility between the two Koreas. He took power exactly as Trump engaged in a verbal escalation with Pyongyang, threatening 'fire and fury' and unilateral military action against North Korea.

NORTH KOREA FIRES ANOTHER INTERCONTINENTAL BALLISTIC MISSILE

As mentioned earlier, Donald Trump's provocative stand further emboldened Kim Jong-un's intent on pursuing his goal of reaching that ultimate capacity to hit the US Mainland whenever he wants.

On Wednesday, the 29th of November 2017, North Korea launched another ICBM that can reach the whole American mainland.

A Korean news agency reported, "With this system, the DPRK has come into possession of another new type of inter-continental ballistic rocket weaponry system, capable of carrying super heavy nuclear warheads and attacking the whole mainland of the US."

US Defence Chief James Mattis, confirmed the missile launch was unprecedented. "It went higher than any previous shot they've taken. It is a research and development effort on their part to continue to build ballistic missiles; to basically threaten everyone in the world."

Donald Trump's response to the launch: "Major additional sanctions will be imposed. This situation will be handled. America has made it clear that it has lost faith in the effectiveness of diplomacy when dealing with Kim Jong-un's communist regime."

Kim Jong-un's response: "The nuclear button is right here on my table."

Donald Trump's response: "It is on my table too and it is a much bigger nuclear button. And it works."

In the Pentagon, senior officers knew that an attack on North Korea could lead to the death of hundreds and thousands in South Korea as well as the North, and would trigger unfathomable global instability. They have reluctantly concluded however, that a pre-emptive US military strike and regime change might be the least harmful option on the menu.

Where will it all lead? That is the question.

THE DOOMSDAY EMBLEMATIC CLOCK

So, where would the Bulletin of Atomic scientists place the needle of the emblematic clock when the scientists meet next.

My guess was that it would not be further away than two minutes to midnight. The closest since 1953.

On 25th January 2018, The Bulletin of Atomic Scientists actually did place the needle of the Emblematic Clock at 2 minutes to midnight. The closest since 1953.

Here is the full text of the bulletin:

"Bulletin of the Atomic Scientists Move Clock Ahead 30 Seconds, Closest to Midnight Since 1953; #Rewind the Doomsday Clock: Cool Trump Nuclear Rhetoric, Negotiate with North Korea, Stick with Iran Deal, Reduce US-Russian Tensions, and Insist on Global Action on Climate Change."

"WASHINGTON, D.C. – January 25, 2018: Citing growing nuclear risks and unchecked climate dangers, the iconic Doomsday Clock is now 30 seconds closer to midnight - the closest to the symbolic point of annihilation that the clock has been since 1953, at the height of the Cold War. The decision announced today to move the Doomsday Clock to two minutes before midnight, was made by the Bulletin of the Atomic Scientists' Science and Security Board, in consultation with the Board of Sponsors, which includes 15 Nobel Laureates. The full text of the Doomsday Clock statement is available at **http://www.thebulletin.org**, and includes key recommendations about how to **#RewindTheDoomsdayClock**.

Video from the Doomsday Clock announcement at the National Press Club in Washington, D.C., is available at **http://clock.thebulletin.org/** and on the Bulletin of the Atomic Scientists' Facebook page at **https://www.facebook.com/BulletinOfTheAtomicScientists/**."

The statement explaining the resetting of the time on the Doomsday Clock notes:

"In 2017, the world leaders failed to respond effectively to the looming threats of nuclear war and climate change, making the world's security situation more dangerous than it was a year ago, and as dangerous as it has been since World War II. The greatest risks last year arose in the nuclear realm. North Korea's nuclear weapons program appeared to make remarkable progress in 2017, increasing risks for itself, other countries in the region, and the United States. Hyperbolic rhetoric and provocative actions on both sides have increased the possibility of a nuclear war by accident or miscalculation. On the climate change front, the danger may seem less immediate, but avoiding catastrophic temperature increases in the long run requires urgent attention now. The nations of the world will have to significantly decrease their greenhouse gas emissions to keep climate risks manageable, and so far, the global response has fallen far short of meeting this challenge."

"Fuelling concerns about the potential of a nuclear holocaust are a range of US - Russian military entanglements, South China Sea tensions, escalating rhetoric between Pakistan and India, and the uncertainty of continued US support for the Iran nuclear deal. Contributing to the risks of nuclear and non-nuclear clashes around the globe, are the rise of nation-state information technology and internet-based campaigns attacking infrastructure and free elections, according to the statement.

Also highlighted as an overarching global concern, is the decline of US leadership and a related demise of diplomacy under the Trump Administration. There has also been a breakdown in the international order that has been dangerously exacerbated by the recent US actions. In 2017, the United States backed away from its longstanding leadership role in the world, reducing its commitment to seek common ground, and undermining the overall effort toward solving pressing global governance challenges. Neither allies nor adversaries have been able to reliably predict US actions or understand when its pronouncements are real and when they are merely rhetoric. International diplomacy has been reduced to name-calling, giving it a surrealistic sense of unreality that makes the world security situation ever more threatening."

In January 2017, the Doomsday Clock's minute hand edged forward by 30 seconds, to two and half minutes before midnight. For the first time, the Doomsday Clock was influenced by statements from an incoming US President, Donald Trump, regarding the proliferation and the prospect of actually using nuclear weapons, as well as those made in opposition to US commitments regarding climate change.

Rachel Bronson, President and CEO of 'Bulletin of the Atomic Scientists' said, "Because of the extraordinary danger of the current moment, the Science and Security Board today moves the minute hand of the Doomsday Clock 30 seconds closer to catastrophe. It is now two minutes to midnight, the closest the clock has ever been to Doomsday, and as close as it was in 1953, at the height of the Cold War."

Lawrence Krauss, Director of the Origins Project at Arizona State University, Foundation Professor at School of Earth and Space Exploration, Physics Department, Arizona State University, and chairperson of Bulletin of the Atomic Scientists' Board of Sponsors, said:

"The current, extremely dangerous state of world affairs need not be permanent. The means for managing dangerous technology and reducing global scale risk exists - many of them are well-known and within society's reach - provided leaders pay reasonable attention to preserving the long term prospects of humanity, and citizens demand that they do so. This is a dangerous time, but the danger is of our own making. Humankind has invented the implements of apocalypse; so it can also invent the methods of controlling and eventually eliminating them. This year, leaders and citizens of the world can move the Doomsday Clock and the world away from the metaphorical midnight of global catastrophe by taking common sense actions."

Robert Rosner and William E. Writher, Distinguished Service Professor in the Department of Astronomy, Astrophysics and Physics at the University of Chicago and Chairperson of Bulletin of the Atomic Scientists' Science and Security Board, said:

"We hope this resetting of the clock will be interpreted exactly as it is meant - as an urgent warning of global danger. The time for world leaders to address looming nuclear danger and the continuing the march of climate change is long past. The time for the citizens of the world to demand such action is now. **#Rewind the Doomsday Clock**."

Sharon Squassoni, Research Professor of Practice at the Institute for International Science and Technology Policy, Elliott School of International Affairs, The George Washington University, and Bulletin of the Atomic Scientists' Science and Security Board, said:

"In the past year, US allies have needed reassurance about American intentions more than ever. They have been forced to negotiate a thicket of conflicting policy statements from a US administration, weakened in its cadre of foreign policy professionals, suffering from turnover in senior leadership, led by an undisciplined and disruptive President, unable to develop, coordinate or clearly communicate a coherent nuclear policy. This inconsistency constitutes a major challenge for deterrence, alliance management and global stability. It has made the existing nuclear risks greater than necessary, adding to their complexity."

Sivan Kartha, Senior Scientist at the Stockholm Environmental Institute and co-leader of SEI's Gender and Social Equity Program, as well as Bulletin of the Atomic Scientists' Science and Security Board, said:

"2017 just clocked in as the hottest year on record that wasn't boosted by an El Nino. And that matches what we've witnessed on the ground. The Caribbean suffered a season of historic damage from exceedingly powerful hurricanes, extreme heat waves struck across the globe, the Arctic ice cap hit its lowest winter peak on record, and the US suffered devastating wildfires. While this was happening, the Trump administration dutifully carried on through the campaign promise of derailing US climate policy, putting avowed climate denialists in top cabinet positions, and announcing plans to withdraw from the Paris Climate Agreement. Thankfully, this didn't cause global cooperation to unravel. Other countries have reaffirmed their commitment to take action against climate change."

#Rewind The Doomsday Clock is the main message of the 2018 statement with the following action steps amongst those recommended:

a. US President, Donald Trump, should refrain from provocative rhetoric regarding North Korea and recognise the impossibility of predicting North Korean reactions. The US and North Korean governments should open multiple channels of communication.
b. The world community should pursue, as a short-term goal, the cessation of North Korea's nuclear weapon and ballistic missile tests. North Korea is the only country to violate the norm against nuclear testing in the last 20 years.
c. The Trump administration should abide by the terms of the Joint Comprehensive Plan of Action for Iran's nuclear program, unless credible evidence emerges that Iran is not complying

with the agreement, or if Iran agrees to an alternative approach that meets US national security needs.

d. Russia and the United States should discuss and adopt measures to prevent peacetime military incidents along the borders of NATO.

e. The US and Russian leaders should return to the negotiation table to resolve differences over the INF treaty, to seek further reductions in nuclear arms, to discuss a lowering of the alert status of the nuclear arsenals of both countries, to limit nuclear modernisation programs that threaten to create a new nuclear arms race, and to ensure that no new tactical or low-yield nuclear weapons are built, even as the existing tactical weapons are never used on the battlefield.

f. US citizens should demand, in all legal ways from their government, action on climate change as it is a real and serious threat to humanity.

g. Governments around the world should redouble their efforts to reduce greenhouse gas emissions, so they go well beyond the initial, inadequate pledges under the Paris Agreement.

h. The international community should establish new protocols to discourage and penalise the misuse of information technology to undermine public trust in political institutions, media, science, and the existence of objective reality itself.

MEDIA CONTACTS: Patrick Mitchell, (703) 276-3266 and **pmitchell@hastingsgroup.com**

UPDATE AS ON END OF APRIL 2018

1. There has been another chemical attack on the city of Douma, on the outskirts of Damascus in Syria, killing about 40 civilians. Russia and Syria have denied any involvement by the Syrian government forces.

2. A few days later, the US, Britain and France carried out surgical strikes on Syrian targets - presumably factories and establishments making chemical weapons - in retaliation to the chemical attacks. There is worldwide criticism of these surgical

strikes, though some countries, notably Japan, Germany and Australia supported the action.

3. Russia, Iran and Syria have started proclaiming victory against the rebels and their supporters. They think the war is over, but the US and UK are trying to say, 'it's not over yet.'

4. Questions are being asked: 'Is there a bomb which is not chemical?', 'Is it ok to kill millions using conventional weapons, but not ok to kill a few dozen rebels against the ruling government (hence equivalent to terrorists) by chemical weapons?'

5. Trump and the North Korean leader Kim Jong-un are likely to meet in May/June to discuss denuclearisation by Kim.

6. CIA Director Pompeo, has already held a secret meeting with the North Korean leader Kim Jong-un.

7. North Korea and South Korea prepare for their own summit on April 27th, in a bid to formally end the 1950-53 Korean War - a major factor in talks.

8. Such discussions between the two Koreas and between North Korea and the United States, would have been unthinkable at the end of last year, after months of escalating tension and fear of war over the North Korea's weapons programs.

9. North Korea and South Korea met on April 27, 2018. They signed the Panmunjomin Declaration of Peace, Prosperity and Unification of the Korean Peninsula. The document commits the two countries to a nuclear-free peninsula and talks about bringing a formal end to the Korean War. The leaders ended the summit with a formal dinner and a toast.

10. Many world leaders were moved by the Korean leaders coming together. The UN General Secretary applauded the historic Korean Summit and noted that many around the world were deeply impressed and moved by the powerful imagery.

What then is likely to be the outcome of the proposed 'Donald Trump - Kim Jong-un' meeting to be held in May/June 2018.

Later the date for the proposed meeting was fixed as 12th June 2018, with Singapore as the venue.

Before I proceed further on what happened in the world during the month of May 2018, I would like to provide an extract from an article that appeared on Google sometime during April 2018, following a Russian claim that they are in possession of Satellite Images that prove that the 9/11 attack was an Inside Job.

CONSPIRACY THEORY ABOUT THE 9/11 ATTACK ON THE WTC TOWERS. EXTRACT FROM THE ARTICLE REFERRED ABOVE:

"Possibly one of the most alleged and widespread conspiracies, is the 9/11 attack in the United States. The United States government has been known (and proven) to have done a multitude of awful things; however, to countries other than its own.

Most know this tale. Some think that the planes never did crash into the Pentagon or the towers, and that it was simply holograms and CGI technology that the government had had for years. Others think that the planes did crash into the towers, but that there was never a plane at the Pentagon, since it was not found on any tapes.

There are demolitionists that claim that certain types of explosives made the towers fall. These people claim to be experts because they use these explosives weekly to take other buildings down.

There are so many glitches and things that just do not seem right about the 9/11 attack, that it is hard to believe that it wasn't an inside job - especially in hindsight.

Many believe that the United States government planned this attack to inspire hatred toward Islam, and in turn Iraq. This would result in the 'War on Terror' which many just see as the 'War of All the Oil We Can Take.' Many American soldiers lost their lives because of this, along with many innocent civilians.

The world may be one step closer to finding the truth of the event from fifteen years ago. The government of Russia claims to have satellite images proving that the 9/11 attack was in fact, an inside job. Putin is threatening the government with this information currently. There is no doubt this is causing mass panic in the White House. Hopefully, the American people will get their answers soon. God knows they deserve to know why so many of their people had to die."

Here I would like to make it clear to the readers, that I am just providing the 'INFORMATION IN THE FIELD' that I am aware of. This information includes my own views – as a Structural Engineer as well as someone who understands a little bit about 'Probabilities and Odds', along with the views of a few others who I reckon are experts in the subject. It is for the readers to judge or speculate on what according to them might have actually happened.
So here we go:

In my view, and I could be wrong, there can be only three possibilities:

1. If the structure is too strong, then the striking object will rebound.
2. If the structure is too weak, then the striking object will pierce through.
3. If the structural frame is neither too strong nor too weak, then the striking object will partly pierce through and partly remain outside. This is expected to be the most likely scenario. But it didn't happen this way. So, it may be a good idea to look at it another way:

We all know that the striking object pierced through, but still the structure didn't collapse immediately. It remained intact for quite some time before the 1000-degree temperature created the fall. The conditions under which this scenario is possible could only be as follows:

a. That the striking object struck at right angles to the structure.

b. That the striking object was small enough height-wise to precisely fit within two successive floor slabs (normally 3.5m in commercial buildings), and came to rest comfortably over the lower slab.

c. That the striking object was small enough in width to pierce through the cladding and the space between two successive exterior columns.

- How do these dimensions compare with the actual size of the plane that was supposed to have hit the tower?
- What then can the conclusion be other than the following:

a. That it was a specially designed plane. The entire operation was extremely well planned and executed with great precision - not once, but twice within the same hour.

b. What then can the other conclusion be except for that it was a joint venture, partly American, partly terrorists – about 80% chance.

c. It was all American, with some help from the terrorists – about 20% chance.

d. That it was all terrorists, with some help from America – less than 1% chance.

The possibility that all four operations that happened within the same hour, were so meticulously planned and so well executed by the terrorists alone without any help from America, is almost zero or as little as 1 in 6 million trillion as can be worked out. I doubt if terrorists of the world had reached this level of intelligence and resourcefulness. In my view, if they were that intelligent, they would have switched to Quantum Physics. A person with that kind of intelligence is unlikely to get negative inspiration from some passages he read from a doctrine written several centuries ago.

And here is yet another alternative: I am completely out of my mind. And I sincerely hope this is the case. I love America, I have great attachments with America. In fact, with every country, perhaps a little bit more for America. I hope it remains 'Great.'

Now these conspiracy theories about the 9/11 attack have been making waves for quite some time. It is also true that they have been 'DEBUNKED' by scientific studies and eyewitnesses.

Besides, it is contended that any conspiracy that needs more than one person for its execution is impossible to hide for long! In an age where we can easily discover what people did in their bedrooms, we would have already seen many coming out to tell the story for the right price.

So, this could be just a part of the Russian Interference in spreading misinformation in order to cause disintegration.

However, many conspiracy theorists who have written in elaborate detail in support of their theories are Americans, not Russians. So, I am asking the question: "What is stopping the Debunkers and the Conspiracy Theorists from coming together in a conference, analysing the whole matter, coming to a consensus, and then informing the world what actually happened?"

For example, here is an extract from what the experts said on the subject:

"We are supposed to believe that both planes were entirely inside the towers with no pieces showing. A Boeing 767 is 156 feet wide and 159 feet long. The distance from the outer perimeter of the North Tower at the alleged point of contact by AA Flight 11, to the central 47 massive inner core beams that are cross-braced, is 60 feet. The distance from the outer surface of the South Tower at the alleged point of contact by UA Flight 175, to the core structure of that building was 37 feet. The difference in length in relation to the North Tower with respect to plane length, and a building length that is measured in terms of the distance to the core structure is about 99 feet. The differential length for the South Tower is approximately 122 feet. A 767 is 159 feet long, so most of the plane has got to be outside of the tower in both cases, since there is simply no room for

the entire length of the plane to crumple into. Why didn't we see 99 feet of AA Flight 11 sticking out of the North Tower or broken off, crumpled up, and/or crumbling to the ground below? Why didn't we see 122 feet of UA Flight 175, sticking out of the South Tower or crumpled up, and/or crumbling to the WTC plaza below?

There is no plane or plane wreckage at all to be seen in the hole of either tower in any video or photo.

Of course, there are no planes to be seen in the holes of either tower or on the street below because, there were no real planes.

We would expect a sharp deceleration as the plane crumpled to fit into the 60 feet of space (North Tower -Flight 11), and 35 feet of space (South Tower - Flight 175), from the perimeter to the central steel core. Instead, in the videos, both planes enter the towers entirely at uniform motion."

None of the 'DEBUNKERS' could explain this.

A friend of mine, that I was in discussion with on Facebook, said this:

"The probe will continue for the next 20 years, as there are thousands of redials in the world and several in America. The word 'Inside Job' will prove nothing, unless it means the Commander-in-Chief did it!! But he looked quite dazed by the news. His first statement after the towers fell was, 'These terrorists have become so diabolical in their attacks to have pulled off something like this in our homeland,' and indeed continued to define it as an act of war by terrorists against America. It now needed a war against Terror itself; in absence of any knowledge of who or where this terror was being transmitted from. So, unless Russia has found any such master transmitter of terror, how does it matter if this transmitter is located inside or outside!! The dilemma will still continue, if you are talking about proving this through some satellite pictures held by Putin!!"

91

My response to my friend's comments:

"Sometimes the Commander-in-Chief himself is unaware of what's happening. And even if the Commander-in-Chief is aware of the plan, acting dazed is no big deal at all. They are good actors, these presidents."

Meanwhile here is another extract from an expert (this time a pilot):

"I flew the two actual aircrafts which were involved in 9/11 - the Flight Numbers 175 and 93. Flight 93 was a 757 that allegedly went down in Shanksville, and Flight 175 was the aircraft that allegedly hit the South Tower.

Like I said, I don't believe it's possible for a terrorist - a so called terrorist - to train on a [Cessna] 172, then jump in a 757-767 class cockpit, vertically navigate the aircraft, laterally navigate the aircraft, and fly the airplane at speeds exceeding its design limit by well over 100 knots, make high-speed high-banked turns, exceeding, probably pulling 5, 6, 7 G's. The aircraft would literally fall out of the sky. I couldn't do it and I'm absolutely positive they couldn't do it.

For a guy to just jump into the cockpit and fly like an ace is impossible – there is not one chance in a thousand," said Wittenberg, recalling that when he made the jump from Boeing 727's to the highly sophisticated computerised characteristics of the 737's through 767's, it took him considerable time to feel comfortable flying.

"The airplane could not have flown at the speeds that they said it did without going into what is called a high- speed stall. The airplane won't go that fast if you start pulling those high G maneuvres at those bank angles. To expect this alleged airplane to run these maneuvers with a total amateur at the controls is simply ludicrous."

"It's roughly a 100-ton airplane. An airplane that weighs 100 tons, all assembled is still going to have 100 tons of disassembled trash and parts after it hits a building."

"There was no wreckage from a 757 at the Pentagon. The vehicle that hit the Pentagon was not Flight 757. We think - as you may have heard before - it was a cruise missile."

As I said earlier, I am just providing the 'Information in the Field' to the extent that is known to me. It is for the reader to make judgements on its authenticity and implications.

"Incidently, there is an American non-profit organization called 'Architects & Engineers for 9/11 Truth' that promotes the 'controlled demolition conspiracy theory, disputing accepted conclusions around the September 11 attacks, including the '9/11 Commission Report'.

Founded in 2006, the group calls for "a truly independent investigation" into the September 11 attacks as they believe government agency investigations into the collapse of the World Trade Center have not addressed what it calls "massive evidence for explosive demolition". As of August 2018, the group has over 25000 members including more than 3000 Architects and Engineers.

However, professional bodies of Architects and Engineers, including Aero-Space Engineers do not support these conspiracy theories. Many mainstream scientists choose not to debate proponents of 9/11 conspiracy theories. Perhaps they do not want to lend them credibility or simply stay away from getting involved."

EVENTS DURING THE MONTH OF MAY 2018

The month of May 2018, witnessed some events of far - reaching consequence. The needle of the 'Doomsday Emblematic Clock'

93

would have seen some wild fluctuations had it been monitored on a daily basis. But I guess the Atomic Scientists will wait and watch for some time, and then announce the shift in the position of the needle - forward or backward - only when there is some sort of clarity in the geopolitical situation of planet Earth. As of now the needle still stands at 'Two minutes to Midnight.'

Here are some of the most significant events that took place during May 2018:

DONALD TRUMP PULLS OUT OF THE IRAN NUCLEAR DEAL

Except for a few countries such as Israel and Saudi Arabia, the entire world condemned the US President's decision to pull out of the Iran Nuclear Deal.

Former President Barack Obama, slammed President Trump's decision to withdraw from the Iran nuclear agreement that Obama had helped negotiate.

The world opinion is reflected in Obama's statement, made on Tuesday, 8th of May 2018. An extract from the same is reproduced below:
"There are few issues more important to the security of the United States than the potential spread of nuclear weapons, or the potential for even more destructive war in the Middle East."

In 2015, Obama and former Secretary of State John Kerry, brokered the so-called Joint Comprehensive Plan of Action limiting Tehran's nuclear program.

"The reality is clear," Obama said on Tuesday: *"The JCPOA is working - that is a view shared by our European allies, independent experts, and the current US Secretary of Defense. The JCPOA is in America's interest, and it has significantly rolled back Iran's nuclear program. The JCPOA is a model for what diplomacy can accomplish. Its inspections and verification regime is precisely what*

the United States should be working on to put in place with North Korea."

"Indeed, at a time when we are all rooting for diplomacy with North Korea to succeed, walking away from the JCPOA risks losing a deal that accomplishes with Iran, the very outcome that we are pursuing with the North Koreans," the former President continued. "That is why today's announcement is so misguided. Walking away from the JCPOA turns our back on America's closest allies, and an agreement that our country's leading diplomats, scientists and intelligence professionals negotiated. In a democracy, there will always be changes in policies and priorities from one administration to the next. But the consistent flouting of agreements that our country is a party to risks eroding America's credibility, and puts us at odds with the world's major powers."

Stressing that "policy debates in our country should be informed by facts," Obama detailed 'six facts', noting that the agreement was reached after building an international coalition that included the United Kingdom, France, Germany, the European Union, Russia, China, and Iran. It has succeeded in "rolling back Iran's nuclear program." The deal is "strictly monitored" by international watchdogs; Iran is in compliance with the agreement; the agreement never expires, and the deal "was never intended to solve all of our problems with Iran."

"We were clear-eyed that Iran engages in destabilising behaviour, including support for terrorism, and threats towards Israel and its neighbors," Obama said. "But that's precisely why it was so important that we prevent Iran from obtaining a nuclear weapon."

He added, *"I believe that the decision to put the JCPOA at risk without any Iranian violation of the deal is a serious mistake."*

Kerry, who has been publicly lobbying for US allies in recent weeks to salvage the agreement, issued his own statement condemning the withdrawal.

"Today's announcement weakens our security, breaks America's word, isolates us from our European allies, puts Israel at greater risk, empowers Iran's hardliners, and reduces our global leverage to address Tehran's misbehaviour while damaging the ability of future administrations to make international agreements," Kerry said. *"No rhetoric is required. The facts speak for themselves. Instead of building on unprecedented non-proliferation verification measures, this decision risks throwing them away and dragging the world back to the brink we faced a few years ago."*

Kerry added, *"The extent of the damage will depend on what Europe can do to hold the nuclear agreement together, and it will depend on Iran's reaction. America should never have to outsource those stakes to any other country. This is not in America's interests. We should all hope the world can preserve the nuclear agreement."*

The leaders of France, Britain and Germany quickly denounced Trump's decision.

POMPEO VOWS 'STRONGEST SANCTIONS IN HISTORY' ON IRAN

Secretary of State Mike Pompeo, vowed on Monday the 21st of May, to levy an 'unprecedented' level of sanctions on Iran, after the US announced it was withdrawing from the 2015 nuclear accord.

In his first major foreign policy address since becoming Chief Diplomat, Pompeo laid out 12 pillars the US would demand from Iran for a new deal, even as he said a new agreement is 'not the objective' of the Trump administration.

RUSSIA CONDUCTED THE WORLD'S LONGEST SURFACE TO AIR MISSILE TEST

US Intelligence sources revealed, 'Russia has test-fired surface-to-air missile 50 miles farther than anyone has before.'

CNBC reported, 'With little fanfare, Russia successfully used a S-500 surface-to-air missile system to hit a target 299 miles away, which is 50 miles farther than any known test.'

Moscow said, 'The system can intercept hypersonic missiles, drones and stealth warplanes like the F-22 and the F-35, and would allow it to destroy targets at near space range.' The test used a modified version of the missile used in the S-300V4 surface-to-air system.

State News Agency reported, 'Russian President Vladimir Putin said earlier in May that he wanted to prepare the S-500 systems for mass production, giving Moscow the ability to engage multiple targets.'

NORTH KOREA THREATENS TO PULL OUT OF THE SUMMIT WITH US PRESIDENT DONALD TRUMP

On 16th May 2018, in an angry statement, North Korea's vice-foreign minister Kim Kye-gwan, accused the US of making reckless statements and harbouring sinister intentions. He pointed the finger squarely at the US National Security Adviser, John Bolton. "We do not hide our feelings of repugnance towards him," Kim Kye-gwan said.

A few days earlier Mr. Bolton had said that North Korea could follow a "Libya model" of verifiable denuclearisation. This alarmed Pyongyang, who watched Libya's Colonel Gaddafi give up his nuclear programme only to be killed by Western-backed rebels a few years later.

Kim Kye-gwan said in his statement that this was "not an expression of intention to address the issue through dialogue".

"It is essentially a manifestation of awfully sinister moves to impose on our dignified state the destiny of Libya or Iraq, who collapsed by yielding their whole country to big powers."

"We do not hide our feeling of repugnance towards Bolton."

Mr. Kim also warned Mr. Trump that if he "followed in the footsteps of his predecessors" - refusing to engage with North Korea unless it gives up its nuclear weapons - "he will be recorded as the most tragic and unsuccessful President compared to his predecessors; far from his initial ambition to make unprecedented success."

The BBC's Laura Bicker in Seoul, opined that North Korea - which had long since said that its nuclear arsenal is essential for its survival as a state - was now making its demands clear. It may pull out of a summit with the US President Donald Trump, if the US insists it gives up its nuclear weapons unilaterally.

The White House responded by saying it was still hopeful that the meeting would go ahead.

"The President is ready if the meeting takes place. If it doesn't, we'll continue the maximum pressure campaign that's been ongoing," said spokesperson Sarah Sanders.
The ground-breaking agreement for Mr. Kim and Mr. Trump to meet came about as North Korea said it was committed to denuclearising the Korean peninsula.

Exactly what that would entail has remained unclear, but North Korea invited foreign media to witness the dismantling of its main nuclear test site later that month.

Why has the North changed its tune? North Korea spent several years building up its nuclear arsenal at enormous cost. The purpose of doing so was its survival. So, to compare denuclearisation in North Korea with Libya or indeed Iraq as John Bolton did, is not going to offer much comfort when it is known that both these regimes collapsed.

This is also a warning shot to the Trump administration. They will be aware of how much Mr. Trump wants this summit, and how it is being spun as a success brought about by his maximum pressure strategy.

There were signs this boasting irritated Pyongyang, but now it has decided to speak out through someone in the position of power.

North Korea wants the world to know that it is coming to the negotiating table from a position of strength, and they may feel that they are making all the concessions.

They've suspended all missile tests and released the three US detainees. Kim Jong-un, met President Moon and the pair signed a declaration. They are about to dismantle a nuclear test site in front of international media.

So, to hear that the Trump administration is claiming credit for a deal they don't like, has been a step too far.

These statements more than hint that North Korea is prepared to walk away from President Trump's summit in Singapore, until they hear a deal they like.

What else does the North's statement say? Mr. Kim's statement, carried by state media said that if "the US corners us and unilaterally demands we give up nuclear weapons, we will no longer have an interest in talks, and will have to reconsider attending the 12th June summit in Singapore." He said North Korea did have "high hopes" but that it was "very unfortunate that the US is provoking us ahead of the summit by spitting out ludicrous statements."

Hours before the announcement, in a sign of growing problems, North Korea also pulled out of a meeting scheduled with South Korea because of anger over the start of US - South Korea joint military drills. North Korea had earlier said it would allow them to go ahead, but then called them "a provocative military ruckus," which was undermining its diplomatic efforts.

The sudden change in tone from Pyongyang is said to have taken US officials by surprise. Analysts said North Korea could be trying to strengthen its hand before talks.

The US state department said it was continuing to plan the Trump-Kim meeting.

A Chinese government spokesman urged North Korea and the US to "meet each other halfway" ahead of their negotiations.

DONALD TRUMP CANCELLED THE 12th JUNE 2018 SUMMIT WITH KIM JONG-UN

On Thursday, 24th of May, President Donald Trump cancelled the scheduled summit in Singapore on the 12th of June with North Korean leader Kim Jong-un, after the recent sparring between the two countries over the planned nuclear talks.

"Sadly, based on the tremendous anger and open hostility displayed in your most recent statement, I feel it is inappropriate at this time, to have this long-planned meeting." Trump wrote in a letter to Kim, which was sent to reporters. Trump's letter also said, "This missed opportunity is a truly sad moment in history." But at the same time, the letter sought to remind Kim of the nuclear arsenal Washington commands. "You talk about your nuclear capabilities, but ours are so massive and powerful that I pray to God they will never have to be used," Trump wrote.

South Korean officials appeared blindsided by the announcement. "We are attempting to make sense of precisely what President Trump means," said spokesman Kim Eui-kyeom, according to Washington Post.
Trump's announcement came hours after North Korean officials threatened to cancel the summit, angered by recent comments from Vice President Mike Pence, and national security adviser John Bolton, who compared North Korea with Libya.

Earlier on Thursday, North Korea announced that it had destroyed the tunnels at what they said was the country's only nuclear test site. Trump did not acknowledge the concession in his letter.

Cracks began to emerge in plans for the summit in the last week, after North Korea threatened to call off the meeting if the Trump administration demanded the country to completely denuclearise. Trump appeared to soften his rhetoric toward North Korea that week, saying that a more gradual option of denuclearisation was a possibility. However, at the same time he made confusing statements about the fate of the summit: "We are moving along. We will see what happens. There are certain conditions we want to put forth. I think we will be able to get those conditions through. And if we don't, we won't have the meeting." Trump had told reporters on Tuesday 22nd May, without specifying what those conditions would be.

The next day, on the 23rd of May, Trump told Fox News there was a "good chance" that the summit would take place.

NORTH KOREA SIGNALLED THAT IT IS STILL OPEN TO TALKS

Late on Thursday, 24th May 2018, North Korea signalled that it is still open to talks with the United States, even after President Trump cancelled a planned meeting with North Korean leader Kim Jong-un.

North Korean Vice Foreign Minister, Kim Kye-gwan, said in a statement that Pyongyang is willing to talk with the US at any point. "We reiterate to the US that there is a willingness to sit down at any time, in any way, to solve the problem," the diplomat said, according to North Korea's state-run Korean Central News Agency.

The North Korean official said that Trump's decision to cancel the June 12th meeting in Singapore was unexpected, arguing the move was not in the world's best interest.

Trump's withdrawal from the meeting also seemed to take South Korean officials by surprise. President Moon Jae-in said he was very perplexed by the decision , and urged Trump and Kim to engage in talks.

KOREAN LEADERS MEET IN A SURPRISE SUMMIT

On 26th May, the North and South Korea leaders met in the demilitarised border area between the two countries.

The meeting was only the second between South Korea's Moon Jae-in and the North's Kim Jong-un. It came as the two sides continued efforts to put the historic US - North Korea summit back on track.

US President Donald Trump, after cancelling the summit scheduled to be held in Singapore on 12th June 2018, later suggested it may still go ahead.

The latest talks were held on the northern side of the Panmunjom truce village, between 15:00 and 17:00 local time (06:00 and 08:00 GMT), Mr. Moon's office confirmed.

"Both leaders exchanged opinions for the successful holding of the North Korea - US Summit," it added, saying that Mr. Moon would announce the outcome of the talks on Sunday morning.
In Washington, the Trump administration spokeswoman, Sarah Sanders, confirmed that an advance team of White House and Department of State officials would leave for Singapore that weekend, as originally scheduled, to prepare for a possible summit there.

THE 12TH JUNE 2018 SUMMIT BETWEEN DONALD TRUMP AND KIM JONG-UN.

They shook hands - tightly of course, and exchanged pleasantries. At first, they met one on one, with no one else other than the interpreters, and later with a larger group of officials from both sides; followed by a working lunch.

A joint statement was prepared and signed by both Trump and Kim. North Korea did make a broad level commitment "to work towards complete denuclearisation of the Korean Peninsula," but the statement was without specific details regarding the item-wise breakdown schedule relating to the dismantling of the nuclear stockpiles; leave aside timelines for the same. The phrase 'denuclearisation of the Korean Peninsula' itself was not clearly defined.

On his part, Trump at a post-summit press conference later, surprised one and all by saying he would suspend the joint US – South Korea war exercises, and in due course of time withdraw the US forces from South Korea. In doing so, he would save a lot of money for the US. This was quite unexpected as he had earlier not consulted on this with South Korean leader Moon, or with his military establishment. But it was music to the ears for Kim Jong-un.

All in all, Kim Jong-un can be considered to be the winner of this first round. He was in the driver's seat the whole time, and made full use of having attained a position of strength with all that nuclear arsenal at his disposal.

Perhaps Iran may get some inspiration from Kim and try to follow the same path.

But was the summit a success?

Sure. A failure of the summit would have led to a possible confrontation. But avoiding mass annihilation was just a one-foot bar for a successful high jump. Avoiding failure of that kind can hardly be called a success. Considering the fanfare, the media attention, and the tremendous amount of significance given to this summit between Trump and Kim, it looked like an attempt being made to resolve a major problem of the human civilization.

What exactly was this problem that needed to be solved?

In my view, the problem was none other than 'TRUMP AND KIM.'

The two people who created the problem by abusing and threatening each other with nuclear strikes, and bringing the doomsday emblematic clock closer and closer towards midnight, suddenly decided to shake hands and solve their own personal problem. This put me in a fix with regards to fixing the location of the needle.

So what can I say, other than this: on a broad level, relating to peace in the region, the picture looks somewhat better than what it was a few months ago - when 'Fire' and 'Fury' were the words in fashion. Substantial credit for this should go to the South Korean President Moon Jae-in, who managed the entire show extremely well. To some extent the credit should also go to Kim for realising and understanding the 'Information in the field' correctly, and making suitable adjustments in his approach to the problem accordingly.

All in all, I would give about 60 % credit to Moon Jae-in, about 30% credit to Kim Jong-un, and about 10 % credit to Donald Trump, who did nothing much except go with the flow. For this meagre act, he congratulated himself endlessly, and bragged and bragged wherever he went.

However, it is too early to say to what extent - if any - the problem relating to denuclearisation of the Korean Peninsula is taken care of.

What about the human rights violations by Kim? I guess this was not in anybody's agenda. As a result, Kim will continue to oppress and depress, not forgetting suppress his own people. There will be no change in this after all, it appears.

THE DOOMSDAY EMBLEMATIC CLOCK

Before I take a call on where to place the needle of the clock, I present below the views of the 'Pugwash Group' on the two important happenings of the last few months.

1. On the US - North Korea Summit:

"The historic first meeting between a sitting US President and the North Korean Leader, was an auspicious first step that provides a good foundation on which to build substantive agreements in the future. Although the summit itself did not produce any dramatic achievements, it nevertheless is an important landmark in the effort to rid the world of nuclear weapons and prevent conflict in North East Asia. The joint statement issued following the meeting was short on commitments. However, mutual confidence building at this time can provide a basis for a process that reduces fear and suspicion, to reverse the spiral of confrontation. However, we caution that past agreements between the US and DPRK have contained similar vague language along with ambiguous commitments and have consequently failed to be respected. We call upon the US and DPRK, as well as other states of the international community who can support these efforts, to engage in a sustained and meaningful diplomatic process that will conclude an agreement on a denuclearised Korean Peninsula and make further efforts to build confidence. This would provide a much-needed success on the road to realise the common aspiration of a world free of nuclear weapons and all other weapons of mass destruction."

2. On the US withdrawal from the Iran Nuclear Deal:

"There are serious threats to the NPT; the most recent and important is connected to the JCPOA, namely the agreement on the Iranian nuclear issue. The decision of the US to abandon the agreement and reinstate heavy sanctions on Iran, could generate serious problems for the NPT in the Middle East. If the other partners of the JCPOA (Russia, China, France, Germany, UK and the European Union), do not oppose the demise of the JCPOA and do not fully commit to keeping the JCPOA alive, then Iran may decide at some point to suspend its membership in the NPT, possibly creating a larger NPT problem in the Middle East, and perhaps even a war in that region."

So where do we place the needle of the Emblematic Clock today, on the 15th of June 2018, as I write these lines? On one hand is a possible peace agreement with North Korea that may rewind the clock by as much as 30 seconds to two and a half minute before midnight, however on the other hand, the US withdrawal from the Iran Nuclear Deal would bring it back to two minutes to midnight. The Bulletin of Atomic Scientists has not made any changes since January 25th 2018. I guess they will review it only after a clearer picture emerges, probably in January 2019.

CURRENT STATUS AS OF SEPTEMBER 2018

ABOUT NORTH KOREA

There is without doubt, a widespread improvement in relations between North and South Korea. It however remains to be seen how this can lead to future negotiations between the US and North Korea.

South Korean President Moon, recently said he has some details to relay to Trump regarding Kim's denuclearisation readiness. But based on public information in the Pyongyang agreement, the Moon-Kim press conference, and Moon's public debrief, the North has not moved the denuclearisation needle forward since the Trump-Kim Singapore summit in June.

ABOUT IRAN

There was an extremely harsh rhetoric from Trump about Iran on Tuesday the 25th of September 2018, at the opening of the 2018 UN General Assembly Meeting. The broad idea is to suffocate Iran, to cripple Iran's economy, and overthrow them. Hammered by the US punitive sanctions—which have triggered a wholesale exodus of foreign companies from Iran since Trump's withdrawal of the United States from the Iran nuclear deal in early May, Iran's options are limited. One of Tehran's few ways of retaliating is to close the Strait of Hormuz (making it nearly impossible for some US allies in the Middle East to ship their oil). Consequently, there is a real danger of war.

For further elaborate details refer to an Article "Iran's Nuclear Crisis" brought out by The Bulletin Of Atomic Scientists.

In short, Iran faces an existential threat from a wealth of adversaries led by the United States, Israel and Saudi Arabia, that could push the country's decision-makers in the direction of nuclearisation.

ABOUT TRADE WARS

"THE BIGGEST TRADE WAR IN ECONOMIC HISTORY BEGINS"

That was the title of a recent blog in "The South China Post."

The US of A, has been relentlessly firing shots of tariffs of hundreds of billions of dollars on China, followed by similar retaliatory measures by China. Neither of them is showing any intention of backing down.

Tariff shots were also fired by America on several other main trading partners including its allies in the post war atlantic trading alliance such as Canada, Mexico, South Korea, Japan and Germany. Some time back Trump called India a Tariff King.

"While a country may try to destroy another by targeting its economy rather than its military, history suggests that a full-blown trade war inevitably leads to a shoot-out between nations," - The South China Post.

At this stage, it appears that if Trump remains POTUS for a few more months, trade wars will escalate into World War III, and ultimately into nuclear wars.

Both world wars were preceded by trade wars. As someone said, 'If goods cannot cross frontiers, armies will.' And as I say, 'If armies cannot cross frontiers, nukes will.'

OCTOBER AND NOVEMBER 2018

The midterm elections were held in the United States in the first week of November. The Democrats have won the House, but the Republicans have retained the majority in the Senate. Commentators in Europe are mostly of the view that the result was not too bad for Donald Trump; some have opined that he could even win the 2020 elections and continue for another term. However, almost all commentators are of the view that Trump is not good for the world.

The murder of the Saudi journalist Jamal Khashoggi at the Saudi Consulate in Istanbul, Turkey, and the CIA's conclusion that the Saudi Crown Prince ordered the killing, could possibly change the equations pertaining to the relations between Saudi Arabia and the US as well as with other countries. The $ 110 billion arms deal between the US and Saudi may be jeopardised, which is bound to upset Donald Trump's calculations. Fact checking revealed that the arms deal is worth only $ 14.5 billion and not $110 billion as proclaimed by Trump. Also, the number of US jobs affected is just about 10000 and nowhere near a million as tweeted by Trump. However, Trump till date is showing no signs of going back on his friendship and deals with the Saudis. This could isolate the US and adversely affect relations with its allies in Europe. At this stage it is hazardous to predict what the final outcome might be.

On the North Korea front, there is no further reduction in the tensile stress. The findings of a Washington think tank reveal that North Korea may be progressing its ballistic missile program at 16 hidden bases.

In the words of CNN's Amanpour, "This has knocked everyone sideways." There is no indication yet that North Korea intends to start denuclearisation, or that the US intends to curtail sanctions on North Korea. No further summit between the US and North Korea is planned in the current year. However, there is no provocative rhetoric from either side. In that respect, the tensile stress is substantially less than what it was during the days of 'Fire and Fury'. But as I said earlier, there is no further reduction in the stress levels since the summit of 12th June 2018.

The Bulletin of Atomic Scientists had their Annual Dinner Meeting at Chicago on 8th November. I happened to be in their mailing list and was consequently invited to the meeting as a delegate. I could not make it, but I had a question to ask pertaining to the mathematical relation (if worked out) between the location of the needle of the emblematic clock and the probability of a nuclear attack taking place anywhere in the world in one calendar year. In short, how serious is 'two minutes to midnight' in comparison with say, 'three minutes to midnight.'

I interacted on email with their Communication Director, Janice Sinclaire, to ask the question. She promptly responded - thanking me for my interest in the Doomsday Clock – and explained that the clock is not a predictor of a nuclear attack. It is rather a metaphor for the end of humanity, and the time is set by taking into account a variety of factors including human-caused climate change and disruptive technologies. She also posted many links to the background on the clock and how it works. These article from the links were quite helpful to me in order to obtain a better overall understanding of the subject.

A recent 'BOAS' article "Will Disruptive Technology Cause Nuclear War" written by Mathew Kroenig and Bharath Gopalaswamy, was quite an eye-opening analysis, showing how new technology might cause nuclear conflict by upending the existing balance of power among nuclear-armed states. This latter concern is more probable and dangerous, and demands an immediate policy response.

Let's say for example that 'x', 'y' and 'z' are the three big powers on the planet Earth - US, China and Russia (not necessarily 'respectively'). Now, consider the possibility that 'x' decides to launch a sophisticated cyberattack against the nuclear command and control 'y', essentially turning off its nuclear forces. Then, 'x' follows up with a massive strike with conventional cruise and hypersonic missiles to destroy 'y's nuclear weapons. Finally, if any forces of 'y' happen to survive, 'x' can simply mop up 'y's ragged retaliatory strike with advanced missile defenses. 'y' will be disarmed and 'x's nuclear weapons will still be sitting on the shelf, untouched.

All this time, 'z' has been watching the proceedings. Now 'z' can do to 'x' what 'x' did to 'y'.

In short, as Putin says, "Whoever leads in AI will rule the world."

So, the solution lies not in preserving second-strike capabilities, but in preserving prevailing power balances more broadly.

Conclusion: In the words of the authors of the article on 'Disruptive Technology', "The consequences of Washington losing the race for technological superiority to its autocratic challengers, just might mean nuclear Armageddon."

SO WHERE WILL THE NEEDLE OF THE DOOMSDAY EMBLEMATIC CLOCK BE WHEN THE ATOMIC SCIENTISTS MEET AGAIN IN JANUARY 2019?

A LOT CAN HAPPEN IN THE NEXT TWO MONTHS.

AS OF NOW, I THINK IT STAYS AT TWO MINUTES TO MIDNIGHT.

THE YEAR 2019 (1A-14)

In January 2019, the Bulletin of Atomic Scientists placed the location
of the needle of the Doomsday Emblematic Clock unchanged at 2
minutes to midnight, the closest since World War 2.

As expected .. Events are happening at break-neck speed .. covered
extensively in my next book ``SWITCHED ON`` about to be published.

 A brief summary of only the highly significant developments of the
last few months is presented below:

The year 2019 can be considered as the year when architects of war
– with the kind help of the Deep State of America and that of many
other countries – are drawing plans for WW3.

Possible candidates – countries - that could be the theatres of war,
are, Iran, Israel, Saudi Arabia, US, Russia, China, Syria, Turkey, Iraq,
etc … not forgetting Pakistan and India.

According to Zarif .. the Foreign Minister of Iran the four B`s were
perfidiously steering the United States toward war with Iran. These
were Saudi Crown Prince Mohammed *b*in Salman, United Arab
Emirates crown prince and de facto ruler Mohamed *b*in Zayed, Israeli
Prime Minister *B*enjamin Netanyahu and White House national
security adviser John *B*olton. The first two, Sunni Arab royals, see
Iran as a regional nemesis; the latter two have made no secret
of their hostility to diplomacy with Tehran and their desire,
instead, for regime change there..

4 oil tanker attacks in the Gulf of Oman in June 2019, followed by
two more in July set the ball rolling for increasing the tensile stress in
the region. 1500 troops were dispatched by the US to the Middle
East. There is no clear evidence who attacked the Oil Tankers.
Washington, Germany, Saudi Arabia and even UK are of the view
that Iran is behind the attacks, and this is being taken as a clear sign

of Iran`s hostile intent. 1,000 additional troops were dispatched to the Middle East. American military planners are well aware of the huge risks of a war with Iran.  But that won`t make the American political leadership to steer the country away from its current confrontational trajectory. As with Venezuela and North Korea, Trump appears to have let Bolton take the lead on Iran, with potentially dangerous consequences.

In August 2019, the Indian Government decided to scrap provisions of Article 370 that gave special status to Jammu and Kashmir, this led to a tense and dangerous situation in the region. The Muslim – majority state of Jammu and Kashmir enjoyed a unique status in predominantly Hindu India for more than 70 years. No more. Both houses of the Indian parliament approved legislation to divide Kashmir into two ``union territories`` and allow non-Kashmiri Indians to move freely into the region, open businesses and buy land. Many Kashmiris feared the result will lead to a wave of migration that ends any hope of Kashmiri independence or autonomy. Pakistan, which has fought three wars with India over Kashmir, reacted with rage, but it wasn`t getting much support from its purported Muslim allies in the Persian Gulf region. At the UN also, Pakistan did not get support from any other country other than China.

There were some - including the Pakistan Prime Minister Imran Khan - who tried to project an alarmist approach to the situation which is far from the ground realities, and promoting violence in India including by their leaders. Addressing a press conference after the UNSC meet concluded, Indian representative said that Pakistan has been trying to mislead the world. China and Pakistan tried to pass their thought as the thought of the world community, but the view of China is not a global opinion. Imran Khan`s rhetoric of a possible nuclear war with India is viewed with serious concern. Articles have been written including one by the `Bulletin Of Atomic Scientists` describing how an India-Pakistan nuclear war might come to pass, and what the local and global effects of such a war might be.

On September 14th, two predawn attacks were carried out on two major oil facilities in Saudi Arabia, knocking out more than half of the top global exporter`s output. Yemen's Houthi rebels claimed responsibility but US Secretary of State Mike Pompeo swiftly accused Iran, which rejected the allegations.

Saudi Arabia, meanwhile, promised to "confront and deal with this terrorist aggression", while US President Donald Trump hinted at possible military action.

On 3rd October, Trump announced withdrawal of US troops from Kurdish-held territory in Northern Syria. This opened up the space for Turkey to attack the Kurds considered by Turkey as terrorists. Turkey`s intent is to drive out the Kurdish presence along the Turkish Syrian Border and resettling Syrian refugees there. About 400 Kurdish Fighters and 70 Kurdish Civilians killed in the Turkish Offensive and more than 130000 displaced.

Kurdish fighters of the Syrian democratic forces who helped - in a big way – the US counterterrorism efforts against ISIS in Syria, are incensed at this atrocious betrayal by US. This led to an   outrage from both Democrats and Republicans in the House and Senate. Republican Senators Mitch McConnell and Lindsay Graham, two of Trump's strongest supporters, both admonished the president for his decision to withdraw troops from Syria. The Turkish offensive opens a wide lane for the resurgence of ISIS in Syria. ISIS detainees escape from the prisons in large numbers. This is likely to present a huge security risk for Europe. Foreign ministers of all 28 EU Member states agree to stop selling arms to Turkey.

Pence and Pompeo meet Turkey`s President Erdogan to broker a 5 day Ceasefire to allow the Kurds to leave ..

And then ..

PUTIN MAKES A STRATEGIC MOVE ON THE CHESSBOARD ..

Putin literally steps in to take center stage ..

Putin meets Erdogan at the Black sea town of Sochi and they plan to carve out a 12000 Sq.km area (400 km long x 30km wide) buffer zone across the Turkish border. Kurds to be driven out from this region called `safe zone`. Russian Troops enter the region from where the US troops left. The zone will be jointly patrolled by the Russian and Turkish troops. Trump removes all sanctions on Turkey.

And so, Erdogan is happy, Putin is happy, Assad is happy, Trump is happy. They are the leaders of nations .. and their happiness counts .. never mind if the common people everywhere are unhappy, , never mind if 400 plus Kurd fighters and 70 plus civilians had to lose their lives, never mind if hundreds of thousands of people had to be displaced, never mind if 1000 plus ISIS prisoners have escaped and are now free, never mind if now there is a distinct threat of an ISIS resurgence.

And so, it's a victory for Trump as emphatically claimed by him, never mind if Its a dramatic setback for US strategic and humanitarian priorities in Syria, never mind if the US is now unable to secure the territorial defeat of ISIS and prevent its resurgence, never mind if the US is now unable to provide a secure space with humanitarian relief for the diverse community of Christians, Kurds and others in the region who have looked to America for support, never mind if the US has now lost its credibility.

I could add another twenty pages to describe what has been going on in the last few months .. in this beautiful planet .. getting ugly.

Suffice to say that :
Its full chaos everywhere. The contamination of the field is in full flow. There is no break in the breaking news in CNN. And its all bad.

Now, the war is on .. and the original deep state (that of Turkey) has joined the other deep states of the world, and together they are all set to create full-fledged chaos on the planet .. not to mention create war fronts at several regions.

And to top it all there is an impeachment enquiry against the president Donald Trump. Fiona Hill, Alexander Vindman, Marie Yovanovitch and many more have shown remarkable courage while standing against the rot in the White House. Come Christmas time in December and the world will know whether Trump will remain POTUS or not. The evidence against Trump is so damning that, if he doesn`t get impeached it will show the American lawmakers and especially Trump`s Republican allies in extreme poor light. Whichever way the result goes, it will have some effect on the World situation. An embarrassed POTUS could possibly do something silly.

SO WHERE WILL THE NEEDLE BE WHEN THE ATOMIC SCIENTISTS MEET AGAIN IN JANUARY 2020 ?

TWO MINUTES TO MIDNIGHT? .. ONE AND A HALF MINUTES TO MIDNIGHT? .. OR .. ONE MINUTE TO MIDNIGHT?

WHAT CAN I SAY .. OTHER THAN THIS .. IT IS TIME TO ACT NOW

That's it - I have placed all the cards on the table and all the information in the field from the year 1905 to November 2019. Now its time for me to make my move, its time for me to play the game of intuition, to make some assumptions, do some calculations, and tell the world what lies ahead for us, if good sense remains elusive.

Chapter Two

What Lies Ahead

WHAT LIES AHEAD FOR THE HUMAN RACE IF GOOD SENSE REMAINS ELUSIVE?

BACK TO THE DOOMSDAY EMBLEMATIC CLOCK

First off, let me try to determine a possible relationship between 'The Location Of The Needle Of The Doomsday Emblematic Clock' and 'The Probability Of A Nuclear Attack Per Year.'

With this I am venturing into a hitherto uncharted territory. I ask the pertinent question: What exactly is implied when the Atomic Scientists say that the emblematic clock is currently at 'X' minutes to midnight.

For example, if we are to determine the probable chance (say 1 in 'Y') of a nuclear attack taking place anywhere in the world in a fixed period of time - say one year. How do we do it when the only information available to us is that the emblematic clock is at 'X' minutes from midnight?

- In short, what is that equation that links 'X' to 'Y'?
- Nowhere in the record books could I find an equation that links 'X' to 'Y'.

In the year 2015, while I was in the process of writing the manuscript of 'Intelligent Field', I carried out a survey by inviting some friends to answer three questions. These friends of mine were reasonably knowledgeable but by no means experts on the subject.

The three questions were:

Q1) What is the probable chance of a nuclear attack taking place
     anywhere in the world, in one calendar year?
Q2) For each nuclear attack, what is the probable chance of a
     global chain reaction, leading to the extinction of the human
     race?
Q3) What is the probable chance that good sense will prevail, and
     there will be no nuclear war in the next 500 years?

25 of my friends responded to the questionnaire. At first, the
arithmetic average of all the answers given by the twenty-five
participants was determined. Higher weightage was given to the
answers that were closest to the arithmetic average, progressively
reducing to lower weightage to the answers which were furthest
from the arithmetic average. In this way, the weighted average
value of the three answers were worked out. They were as follows:

Answer to Q1   -   1 in 300
Answer to Q2   -   1 in 12
Answer to Q3   -   1 in 10

In general, the participants were more optimistic that good sense
will prevail, and had faith in the human instinct of self-preservation.
Their optimism corresponded more likely to a value of 'X' as 5
minutes before midnight, even though the official value as per the
Bulletin of Atomic Scientists at the time of the survey
corresponded to 'X' as 3 minutes before midnight.

Thus 'Y' was equal to 300, and corresponded to a value of 'X' as 5
minutes before midnight.

Hence, the conclusion was 'Y' in figures is equal to 'X' in seconds.
Or 'Y' = 60 'X', if 'X' is in minutes.

So, if 'X' = 2 minutes as on date, as per the current status of the
Bulletin of Atomic Scientist, then 'Y' is worked out as 120.

117

Which means the probable chance of a nuclear attack taking place somewhere on the planet Earth in one year is 1 in 120 i.e., 0.83 percent.

THE EXTENT OF DANGER TO THE WORLD IF GOOD SENSE DOES NOT PREVAIL

Recall the atomic bombs that were dropped on Hiroshima and Nagasaki which caused 130,000 deaths instantly, and several thousand more deaths due to radiation. The modern bomb is about 2,500 times more powerful than the ones dropped on Hiroshima and Nagasaki. Only about one hundred of these - if dropped as uniformly distributed across the planet - are enough to obliterate the human race. We have about twenty thousand of these at our disposal, and not all of them are in safe hands.
Unless good sense prevails, there is extreme danger to humanity. A solid consensus for reversing reliance on nuclear weapons is required as a vital contribution to preventing the chance of them going into potentially dangerous hands, and ultimately ending up as a threat to the world.

EXTINCTION PROBABILITIES

Now consider the answer to Q2, according to which there is a 1 in 12 chance of a nuclear attack leading to a global chain reaction, strong and powerful enough to lead towards the extinction of the human race. Based on this value of answer to Q2, the probable chance of extinction of human race - per year, is worked out as 1 in 120*12, i.e. 1 in 1440.

Accordingly, the chances of survival from extinction is worked out as 1439/1440 %, i.e. 99.93 %.

Assuming the emblematic clock needle stays at an average location of two minutes to midnight for the next one thousand years, and the probable chance of each nuclear attack leading towards a global chain reaction causing extinction of the human race remains at 1 in 12 for the next one thousand years, the probability of extinction of human civilization is worked out as $1 - (1439/1440)^{1000} = 0.50$, i.e. 50%.

Corresponding value (probability of extinction) for the needle staying at one minute to midnight for the next one thousand years is worked out as $1 - (719/720)^{1000} = 0.75$, i.e. 75% chance of extinction.

Corresponding values - extinction probabilities, for the needle staying at three/four/five minutes to midnight, can be worked out as 37%, 29%, 24% respectively.

It is reasonable to assume that the needle of the emblematic clock may fluctuate between '1 minute to midnight' and '5 minutes to midnight'.Accordingly it is reasonable to assume that the probable chance of the human race getting extinct within the next one thousand years varies between 24% and 75 %.

SO, I MAKE MY MOVE - MAKE KNOWN MY ASSUMPTION

I assume, regardless of what happens in the remaining part of the calendar year 2018, that on an average for the next one thousand years, the needle of the emblematic clock stays at 3 minutes to midnight.

With this assumption, I venture to predict a 37% chance of extinction of the human civilization within the next one thousand years.

The maximum danger is in the next two centuries, with the chance of extinction being about 12 percent. As the years pass and the intelligence in the field keeps rising, the probabilities of extinction keep reducing to 10 percent between years 2200 & 2400; to 7 percent between years 2400 & 2600; to 5 percent between years

119

2600 & 2800; and to 3 percent in the last two centuries of the current millenium.

Will it be safe after that? What about the next thousand years and the next thousand after them?

Hopefully, the chance of extinction could progressively reduce to 14 percent, then 8 percent, then 5 percent, then 3 percent, millennium-wise.
That means there is a survival chance of $(0.63*0.86*0.92*0.95*0.97) = 46$ percent after fifty centuries; thus an extinction chance of nearly 54 percent in the next fifty centuries. Again, hopefully, about 8 percent in the next fifty.

That's it; we should be safe thereafter.

THE FINAL CONCLUSION

Unless good sense prevails, the chance of survival of the human race from self-destruction is less than 40%.

Is that scary?

Well, it's not as scary as what Stephen Hawking thought. According to him, we have only about two hundred years left, and we should shift to another star system before that. Martin Rees is even more pessimistic and thinks this is our final century.

Some people might call it a crude way of working, but I'll be glad to know if there is a better way. The trouble is, no one is really doing any sort of calculation on this extremely important issue. Frankly, not many people in the world are really bothered about what lies ahead for the human race; which is the real tragedy.

IMPLICATIONS OF EXTINCTION

All the billions of souls are out in the open. Perhaps stranded in the Interstellar space. No human beings anywhere, no environment or biochemistry available for obtaining human consciousness. Should they wait patiently for that biochemistry to evolve again, or lose patience and hitchhike to another star system and hope for the best.

Or maybe, get inside termites. There is plenty of food available such as the woodworks, even concrete.

A chilling thought nevertheless.

What's more, the 'Cosmic Mind' will not come to our rescue.

Chapter Three

Information As The Definition Of Reality

Notwithstanding the random movements of the quantum-level particles, the fact however remains, that the thoughts in our minds do make a difference in how the matter in our body behaves. So, where is the link between the quantum and the classical? I believe the 'Intelligent Field' is that link.

To drive home the point made above pertaining to the intelligent field and its linkage with the information in the field, I respond with some quotations from two of my favourite books dealing with the subject of information theory: 'Information and the Nature of Reality', edited by Paul Davies and Niels Henrik Gregersen, and 'The New Quantum Age,' by Andrew Whitaker.

So, here we go:

Quotation 1: *"The content that constitutes mind is not in the brain, nor is it embodied in neuronal processes in bodies interacting with the outside world,"* Terrence. W. Deacon (3A-01).

Response: What is implied - and I am in agreement with it - is that the "I" that is identified with my brain, does not include a mind of its own. That mind is not the exclusive property of the "I" of the brain. That mind is available to all the "I"s of all brains and is common to all. It is always on the lookout for an appropriate biochemistry to give itself consciousness and life. We all have the same mind; it is just that our consciousness is always in the singular.

Quotation 2: *"The very first information processing revolution, from which all other revolutions stem, began with the beginning of the universe itself. The big bang at the beginning of time, consisted of huge numbers of elementary particles, colliding at* *temperatures of billions of degrees. Each of these particles carried with it bits of information, and every time two particles bounced off each other, those bits were transformed and processed. The big bang was a bit bang."* Seth Lloyd (3A-02).

Response: Yes, indeed this universe of ours is a simulated universe. Who or what caused the simulation? The best bet I think, is an all-pervading intelligent field, or the omnipresent infinite mind; which is omnipresent in space as well as in time.

Quotation 3: *"I could draw you a map of all the tens of thousands of components in a single-celled organism and put all the proper arrows connecting them (and even then) I or anybody else would look at that map and have absolutely no ability whatsoever to predict anything."* Jesper Hoffmeyer (3A-03).

Response: But when we consider the cell as a whole, such as a single-celled paramecium as it swims towards food, we can very well predict that there is a good probability that en route, it will retreat from danger, negotiate obstacles, and achieve its goal. Of course, our ability to make these predictions is based on the information available to us, which in turn, is based on observations of the past. But what can the explanation for this be?

Now, consider the information carried by DNA molecules.

Quotation 4: *"The code does provide a program for constructing an organism, but no person has constructed it, and no consciousness needs to understand and apply the program. It has originated by ordinary evolutionary processes, and like a computer program, it operates without the need for conscious interpretation."* Keith Ward (3A-04).

Response: One can of course argue that consciousness is just a random by-product of the evolutionary process. However, where does the intelligence that determines the code that provides a program for constructing that organism come from? What can be the explanation for this? Indeed, we need a holistic cosmic explanation, in which the development of the parts is explained by their contributions to the existence of an integrated totality.

Quotation 5: *"Taken together, these considerations suggest the idea of a primordial consciousness, that is ontologically prior to all physical realities, that contains the coded information for constructing any possible universe, and that can apprehend and appreciate any physical universe that exists. It would certainly be a strong reason for creating a universe that might contain finite consciousness, that could share in appreciating, and even in creating some of the distinctive values potential in the basic structure of the universe. Whether or not one calls such a primordial consciousness 'God' is partly a matter of taste." Philip Clayton (3A-05).*

Response: No harm will be done to our psyche or our ego, if we call this primordial consciousness an intelligent field or maybe an infinite mind. This intelligent field has evolved over the years and is still evolving.

Quotation 6: *"The recent developments in physics (nonlocality in particular), briefly summarised here provide a powerful empirical refutation of a materialistic world view."*

(This seems to say that reality is more like energy than matter.)

"The conundrums are not resolved by turning one's back on the mysterious nature of objects and particles in physics. What is necessary, I suggest, is that we pursue this path of natural science as far as it can take us. Neither over quick leaps into metaphysics, nor refusing to acknowledge the complex philosophical issues raised by today's science will help." Philip Clayton (3A-05).

Response: I couldn't agree more with Philip Clayton. Scientists, philosophers and theologians must be partners, and should have a common ground in understanding and formulating an adequate post materialistic theory of the natural world.

Quotation 7: *"Quantum mechanics then demolished the concept of an external state of reality in which all meaningful physical variables could be assigned well-defined values at all times. So, a subtle shift occurred, at least among theoretical physicists, in which the ground of reality first became transferred to the laws of physics themselves, and then to their mathematical surrogates, such as Lagrangians, Hilbert spaces, and so on. The logical conclusion of going down that path is to treat the physical universe as if it simply 'is' mathematics. The traditional relationship between mathematics, physics and information may be expressed symbolically as follows:*

MATHEMETICS□PHYSICS□INFORMATION Paul Davies (3A-06).

Response: Indeed, mathematics is the president of the company called the universe. There are many such laws in which mathematics gives orders on how to proceed, and they were well-crafted with nicely designed constants to create good enough probabilities for lives and consciousness to evolve at millions of locations, and for theoretical physicists to arrive and then understand these laws.

Laws, such as the uncertainty principle, in which mathematics plays a trick that does not allow the quanta to get created out of nothing except for the shortest possible, and thus most irrelevant, period of time.

Laws, such as quantum entanglement, in which mathematics plays a trick that permits entanglement but does not permit information to be sent faster than at the speed of light.

Both these tricks have been played out by the mathematician by incorporating certain randomness in the nature of reality. In the former case, the vacuum randomly fluctuates between being and nothingness, while in the latter, the mathematician keeps shuffling the deck of nature in such a way that the randomness remains intact.

I should go as far as to say that randomness is the vice president. Then, at the center of everything, there is this thing called equivalence. It is the cleverest of all the laws; it goes without saying that this law is out-and-out mathematics, and physics is just dancing to its tune.

Paul Davies is one of my heroes. I have read his books and have written about him in 'Six Words.'

Quotation 8: *"Decoherence effects are the basis both of the mechanism whereby our thoughts can affect our actions and of the reconciliation of quantum theory with our basic intuitions. The quantum state of the brain is reduced to a collection of parallel potentialities, each of which is essentially a classically conceivable possible state of the brain. Your physically described brain is an evolving cloud of essentially classically conceivable potentialities."* *Henry Stapp (3A-07).*

Response: These lines are of far-reaching significance; they remind of the following lines by Roger Penrose:

'Probabilities do not arise at the minute quantum level of particles, atoms, or molecules. These evolve deterministically, but seemingly via some mysterious larger-scale action connected with the emergence of a classical world that we can consciously perceive.' *(3A-08).*

Here too, I link it with the 'Intelligent Field' which I consider the guiding force that links the quantum with the classical.

For example: Consider that I am just walking in the rain along a road, and I need to turn left at the next turn to go to my destination.

126

Now, the quantum entities inside my body keep moving here and there at random, with complete disregard to the phenomenon of cause and effect. They however, will (in their trillions) be at the right places at the right time to ensure that I am turning left and not going straight or turning right. And in case something happens to me before I turn left, such as my getting hit by a car or something, the classical world (of the car hitting me) informs the quantum world of the changes in probabilities, and the quantum particles inside me will be at the right places at the right times to make sure that I fall down, provided (of course) that the impact of the car was sufficient for the purpose.

Quotation 9: *"The resurrected Jesus Christ is not the resuscitated pre-Easter Jesus of Nazareth. The entirety of Jesus's life, his charisma and his power, is presence and efficacious in the resurrected and exulted one. The complete fullness of his person and his life is now present 'in spirit and faith,' but this is hard to comprehend to naturalistic and scientific thought." Michael Welker (3A-09).*

Response: The subject needs to be viewed in the context of the information theory. There is no doubt that the presence of such information in the field that gives solace and peace of mind in prayer and in the knowledge of Jesus's presence (in whatever form one can imagine), is very much helpful to mankind. However, when it is a question of "talking science" and discussing the subject in the context of its correlation with the information theory, we must ask the question: is resurrection a possibility? Why is it assumed that the answer provided to this question by a naturalist or a scientist will be different from that provided by a theologian? Particularly in the light of the fact that the information - the data that constitutes the input to perform their analysis - available to all of them is the same in all respects. Indeed, we must follow the teachings of the great religious leaders of the past, but there should be no reason to believe the events of rising from the dead, or walking on water.

All in all, when we talk science, the nature of reality is just information - the information in the intelligent field or the infinite mind. We may call this intelligent field or infinite mind our "god", but this god is just a computer. No doubt it is intelligent; it gives us everlasting consciousness (everlasting in the sense that we are unconscious of our 'unconscious tenures' so they pass quickly), it designs our bodies and their capacities to grow, and above all, it designs the laws of the universe with precisely calculated mathematical constants. However, this intelligence in the field is limited to the sum total of information acquired and processed through time. The quantum of intelligence is, of course, powerful enough to sustain the universe, which is impressive, but whether or not we can call it "divine" is a matter of taste. We must take into consideration the fact that many times, life can only live at the expense of other life and that most living creatures kill each other in everlasting strife.

Quotation 10: *"There are only four problems that the scientists have not been able to solve so far. These are:*

1. *How to combine quantum theory and general relativity to produce a single theory (of quantum gravity) that can claim to be a complete theory of matter.*
2. *How to combine all the particles and forces in today's physics to give a theory as manifestations of a fundamental unity.*
3. *To explain how the values of the free constants in the standard model of particle physics (the masses and life times of the various elementary particles) are chosen in nature.*
4. *To explain the existence and properties of dark matter and dark energy.*

The above four problems will not be solved in isolation; the solution of these great problems will come together. A possible way forward is to give up the attempt to apply quantum theory to the universe as a whole, and to regard quantum theory as the record of quantum information that one subsystem may have about another subsystem, as a result of their mutual interaction. In this way, ideas from the study of quantum information may demonstrate how elementary particles may emerge from quantum space-time." Lee Smolin (3A-10).

Response: In other words, the universe as suggested by scientist Seth Lloyd, can be considered to be a quantum computer. One may ask the question "but what does the universe compute?" Lloyd gives the answer: "It computes its own behavior. At first, the patterns it produces are simple, but as it processes more and more information, it produces more intricate and complex patterns on the physical side, giving rise to galaxies, stars and planets, while on the human side, it produces life, language, human beings, society and culture."

They say that a classical computer cannot simulate a quantum mechanical system; so the universe being quantum mechanical, cannot be considered a classical computer and can only be a quantum computer. My own idea is that all this happens in a field, and when sufficient information is accumulated in the field, it becomes an intelligent field. When the intelligence in the field keeps increasing (like that of an infinite mind), it is focused on creating biochemistries suitable for building awareness and consciousness to understand itself. Hence, that portion of the computation which the universe does, which is attributed to the intelligence of the intelligent field, is not completely in the domain of quantum computation. To some extent, it could even be called classical computation.

It could also be that the intelligent field is itself a product of simulation, which then simulates the universe. And it goes on and on, step by step, with trillions and trillions of intermediate steps, through trillions of years and countless eons of the universe. It could be that we, the human beings, are an intermediate step. This point of view also encapsulates the anthropic principle, and explains what happens when a new aeon of the universe is created. All the information is available in the field; all the

129

constants of nature are already known to the intelligence in the field. It is just the "switching on" that is needed. Whether to call it an intelligent field or an infinite mind or "God" is just a matter of taste. The theists can call it "God" while the atheists should be happy to call it the intelligent field or an intelligent mind. The dispute should end.

Quotation 11: *"Mind has a central place in the ultimate nature of reality." John C. Bell*

Response: I guess this is the 'Infinite Mind' of the 'Intelligent Field'. Yes indeed, Mind and Consciousness have a central place in the ultimate nature of Reality; never mind whether the said idea is not professionally useful to contemporary scientists, or practically useful to build machines. It can be philosophically useful to unite science with religion, to unite people, cultures and religions, to end conflicts and wars and so on.

CONCLUSIONS:

So, it boils down to this.

I believe this Universe of ours is a simulated universe, a quantum computer that keeps processing 'Information' all the time. It is this 'Information in the Field' that is responsible for what happens in the universe. The current information in the field shows large scale contamination that is potentially dangerous for the human civilization. Time is running out for us. It is high time we delete all that evil and dangerous information, and flood the field with good information about love and peaceful coexistence. No 'God' of any kind will come to our rescue. We need to create probabilities for our survival on our own. It is high time for 'GOOD SENSE' to prevail.

Chapter Four

Good Sense Must Prevail

An integrative approach is required to ensure that nuclear wars are completely avoided. But time for this is running out.

A major intellectual effort is required to bring forth checks and balances to ensure safety and security of human beings from incompetent and egoist leaders of nations. Intelligent minds of the world must come forward to provide that intellectual effort.

WHAT EXACTLY IS GOOD SENSE?

"Avoidance of extinction must be the most important subject to be taught in universities worldwide."

Now there are many ways in which human civilization can get extinct, such as a major asteroid hitting the earth, bio engineered diseases, extreme climate change, nuclear wars, etc.

A large sized asteroid hitting the Earth can possibly cause extinction of the human race, but the chances of a major asteroid hitting the Earth in the next ten thousand years is probably less than one in about hundred thousand. By that time, technology would have improved substantially to be able to deflect the course of the incoming asteroid by a nuclear strike or something.
bio engineered diseases and extreme climate change, etc., can lead to tens of millions of people experiencing painful deaths, but is unlikely to cause complete extinction of the human race.

That leaves us with nuclear wars and possible global chain reactions as the most dangerous and the most likely causes of extinction of the human race. I guess, we should be focused on this.

As worked out earlier - even if it was a crude way of working - there is a sixty percent chance of the human race getting extinct within the next ten thousand years. This, I think, is a rather optimistic assessment. There are many scientists and writers who think we do not have that much time. Stephen Hawking was of the opinion that we have only a few centuries at our disposal, and within these few centuries we need to shift to another planet; perhaps of another star system. Martin Rees is even more pessimistic and thinks this is our final century.

We have seen the consequences of extinction of the human race. There will be no more generations of human beings in the future.

It would mean the end of an elegant story of evolution, which has already led to an extraordinary, intelligent life that has made and is still making substantial progress. In about a hundred thousand years we have become men from apes, and there is every likelihood that in a similar period of time or even before that we may all become super minds, provided we can survive. If we fail to prevent our extinction, we will have blown the opportunity to create something truly wonderful.

The planet Earth is a unique and wonderful place to live in as a human being. It has the potential to remain habitable for as many as a few billion years. There will be ample time for our species to colonise the galaxy. Getting extinct would mean a GREAT OPPORTUNITY LOST.

Should we not do something about it?

Now, I do not mean to say that nothing has been done in this regard.

We have survived through the cold war and substantially scaled back our reserves of nuclear weapons. The Pugwash Movement has been immensely helpful in this regard.

But is that enough?

I would say: NO, IT IS NOT ENOUGH.

The emblematic clock keeps moving closer and closer to midnight.

The big problems are not getting solved.

The big conflicts between nations are not getting resolved. They are in fact getting aggravated.

Should we not do something about it?

Surprisingly, rather astonishingly, no one is doing anything about it.

No one is going deep into the problem and trying to analyse it.

No one is even taking measurements to determine the extent of the damage done. Of course, the 'Bulletin of Atomic Scientists' are doing an excellent job of tracking the needle of the emblematic clock. But even they have not clearly spelt out what it means when they say that the emblematic clock stands at two minutes to midnight.

No books are being written on the subject. At least, I am not aware of such books.

Except for 'INTELLIGENT FIELD' written by yours truly.

This book is significant for world peace. It should set the stage for world leaders to come together and address the nuclear issues before they get out of control. The future and security of the human race should not be left to the revolving doors of chance. It has to be planned meticulously with no scope for miscalculations. Dialogue on an international level needs to be launched within the framework of the Nuclear Non-Proliferation Treaty. All the

133

important nations of the world, regardless of whether they have nuclear weapons or not, must participate in the dialogue, and cover the entire range of issues related to the elimination of nuclear weapons. All participants of the dialogue should understand the problems of the world from a neutral (global) perspective, and not from the perspectives of this or that nation or religion. They should then adopt an integrated approach to resolve the problems. There is no doubt that all this requires a major intellectual effort. But there is no dearth of beautiful minds on the planet who can achieve this.

Once we are out of the current dangerous time zone, we will see what the intelligent field has in store for us. The philosophical ideas of an 'Intelligent Field' and of the 'Travelling Cosmic Mind', as elaborately explained in the book, have added a significant new dimension to the quest for knowledge on Philosophy, Religion, Spirituality, Humanism, and other similar paths, towards formulating an approach to life that can certainly ensure a bright future for the human race.

The invisible 'Intelligent Field' with its ever-increasing information, is in control of what happens in the universe. The processing of information is a continuous activity. The universe appears to be a quantum computer that computes its own behaviour. At some stage in the remote past, 'Intelligence' may have arrived in the field and started processing the information in ways to bring in life and consciousness to understand itself. In the present aeon of the universe, the permanence of consciousness appears to be ensured by the idea of a travelling cosmic mind that travels forwards and backwards in time to always remain in the Stelliferrous Era of the universe where stars are shining, where life and consciousness is flourishing. It does not travel to the infinitely long Dark Eras of deep future where no consciousness is available to it.

However, there is nothing divine about the 'Intelligent Field' or about the 'Travelling Cosmic Mind'. The scope of work is limited to

134

searching for an appropriate biochemistry, and obtaining consciousness in whatever form it is available.

The 'IF' or the 'TCM' is unlikely to come to our rescue.

It is up to us to create probabilities for our survival. The subject must be understood from a neutral perspective. Some out of the box thinking is required to save us from extinction.

THE 'COMPASSION' (MORAL AND ETHICAL) INDEX 'QC' OF LEADERS OF NATIONS

The subject must be understood from an unbiased perspective.
How would a neutral figure, such as a being from outer space (let's call him "F"), who has watched all the proceedings and has complete knowledge and understanding of all the conflicts on planet Earth, address the problems in a way that is acceptable to all concerned as far as possible? It is assumed, of course, that "F" understands human nature, and is perfectly aware that a typical human being, anywhere in the world, wants to live in peace. It is also assumed that the average moral standard is the same in all countries and does not differ from country to country, as it is not a measure of "temperature" or "humidity". The average quotient Q_c (Compassion Index), pertaining to the desire to "live and let live" is also generally the same for all countries. It is a requirement for peace in the world that the corresponding quotient "Q_c" pertaining to the leaders of nations, must be well above the average "Q_c" of that nation. The reason behind conflicts and wars, particularly civil wars, is that it is not the case in some countries. It is the interactions of the world that lead to the coming together of millions of atoms and molecules, becoming a speck of jelly, and it is the same phenomenon that is responsible for the said speck of jelly to go on to become either Hitler, Gandhi, Einstein, you or me. The same phenomenon is responsible for some leaders of nations ending up with "Q_c" substantially below the required level.

With all this, it does not serve the purpose if we call a certain country, which is just a geographical area, a terrorist state and another country in another geographical area, "selfish and arrogant," when we know that it is the leaders of these nations (having low "Qc") who must be held responsible for bringing their nations to such disrepute. However, the common man should not suffer on account of the low "Qc" value of his country's leaders.

Therefore, "F" should first understand how the common man from each country finds himself entangled in these complex and dangerous situations through no fault of his, and how he can be extricated from these entangled states.

Thus, the main requirement in the analysis is to identify the leaders of nations who have a negligible "Qc", who could be dangerous to the world, particularly so if they have access to nuclear arsenal.

As an example, to drive home the point that I am making, consider the case of Adolf Hitler, whose "Qc" was always extremely low. If Germany had won the race towards the first use of the atomic bomb, it is distinctly possible that he would not have limited himself to just a couple of strikes. It is quite likely that he may have struck multiple times in multiple countries and caused catastrophic damage worldwide. As it happened, Germany was defeated in the war and Hitler was about to commit suicide. At this stage, when his "Qc'" would have almost reached the level of zero, had he come into possession of the same nuclear arsenal that Germany now has, he would have surely made full use of it and would have perhaps destroyed the human civilization.

It can happen in the future. In the not-too-distant future; the nuclear arsenal can move into the wrong hands, the hands of terrorists, and can increase their power and capacity to cause damage. But substantially more dangerous than that is the distinct likelihood of powerful hands making wrong use of the arsenals that are already in their possession.

The available nuclear arsenal in the world is several hundred times more than the quantity required to destroy the entire human race, with each of the five most powerful nations in possession of more than fifty times the required quantum to obliterate civilization.

THE ESSENCE OF RELIGION

The Compassion Index "Qc" of the leaders of nations, must also take into account their understanding of the 'Essence of Religion'.

Religion, as we all know is manmade; it is a product of the human brain. Adjustments need to be made to global religious thinking, in order to suit the current geopolitics of the world, if we want to save the human civilization from self-destruction. An integrated approach towards the convergence of religions to end religion-based conflicts and wars is necessary.

We need to be religious only to the extent of following the essence of the religion, and not be concerned about which religion it is. The essence of religion should be:

a.   To find solace and peace of mind in prayer and/or meditation.
b.   To live and let live.
c.   To be compassionate and understanding.
d.   To take care of the environment around us.

There is nothing Hindu, Muslim, Christian, or Buddhist about the essence of religion; just as there is nothing Greek about the Pythagorean Theorem.
The essence of religion as defined above is regarding the practice of religion but when it is a question of understanding god and reality, then we are talking about religious philosophy.

Here, it is my considered view that religion must converge with science, keeping in mind that the established truths of science should not be violated. Which would imply that an anthromorphic

137

(physical function) God, is unlikely to be the form in which God exists. It is of course to be noted that moral and ethical values are outside the realm of science, whereas they are all very much in the realm of religion. At the same time, if the religious view (as spelt out in various religious doctrines), teaches us that moral and ethical values were the word of God, then the question arises - if there is no such physical (made up of atoms and molecules) 'God', can we say that the moral and ethical values we talk about are wrong? No, we cannot. These morals and values have survived - almost intact - over the years. So, it appears that science and moral questions are quite independent; however, an understanding of both is required to make sound judgements.

If 'THIS' happens, then 'THAT' is likely to happen (as determined by Science), and if 'THAT' is not a desirable outcome (as determined by Religion on Moral and Ethical grounds), then 'THIS' should not be permitted to happen.

It all boils down to the 'Information in the Field' and its implications. Hence, the entire subject relating to convergence of science with religion needs to be viewed in the context of the "information theory".

The presence of information on religions of the world, including that of mythology and religious philosophy, that leads people to churches, temples, masjids, etc., or to perform rituals that provide solemnity to occasions such as marriages and festivals, has over the years, given immense happiness, solace, and peace of mind to the people of the world. There is no reason why they should not continue to do so. However, one should realise that the presence of certain information in religious doctrines, which permits intolerance and violence against other religions, is full of self-endangerment and destructive potential. It has, over the years, caused religious extremism, conflicts and wars. There is no reason to believe that these doctrines should not be reformed.

If the doctrines contain passages that incite violence, they cannot be considered as religious teachings for the simple reason that they do not conform to the Essence of Religion (EOR). There is no doubt that the composers of these passages did not have religion as motivation; perhaps the motivation was none other than obtaining power over people and resources. It all boils down to the fact that the 'Qc' of these leaders was extremely low.

But who is to reform these doctrines? That is the question. At this stage, there exists no authority to do so, and this is attributable to the fact that there exists no consensus to do so. For a consensus to be obtained, the various factions of the concerned religion first need to be united in all respects, and have a uniform ideology that is conforming to the EOR as outlined earlier. The religious leaders should then assemble in an international conference where leaders of other religions are also present. The objective of this conference should be to appropriately reform the doctrines in a way that is acceptable to all religions and can lead toward convergence. The outcome should be well publicised by the media across the world. It should also cover the topic of rehabilitation of the misunderstood human beings (some people call them "terrorists" but I call them 'Victims of Time'). These people should be open to thoughtful programs that would improve their material well-being, and they should be informed out of their irrational beliefs by dialogue, persuasion and education.

THE 'INFORMATION' (KNOWLEDGE AND INTELLIGENCE) INDEX 'QI' OF LEADERS OF NATIONS

Complete 'Information in the Field', relating to a comprehensive and up to date knowledge and understanding of the geopolitical situation on the planet Earth - particularly in the nuclear field - must be at the fingertips of all leaders of nations. Three conferences were held in the month of June 2018 by the Pugwash Group. The concluding paragraph extracted from a paper prepared by the Secretary General of Pugwash, Paulo Cotta Ramusino, as given below is pertinent.

"The strengthening of the NPT (and now, the preservation of the JCPOA), the creation and consolidation of NW (or WMD) free zones, the improvement of NPT-related mechanisms (making the NPT Review Conferences more efficient, enforcing control by the IAEA of civilian nuclear activities), the widening of membership in the NBT, and progress towards the entry into force of the CTBT, are all parts of a global effort to reduce the role of nuclear weapons, to highlight the dangers for mankind represented by these weapons, and to move towards a more secure global environment."

All leaders of nations are required to have read all the papers, and articles, issued by the Pugwash Group as well as by the 'Bulletin of Atomic Scientists' during the last few decades, or preferably since their inception.
All leaders of nations are required to have complete knowledge and in depth understanding of all the conflicts on planet Earth, including the conflicts between nations, as well as within nations, i.e. civil wars. This requires an in depth understanding of the root cause of these conflicts, as well as thorough knowledge and understanding of the methodology to be adopted for their resolution, from a human perspective, and not from the perspective of any nation or religion.

EXAMPLES:

a. Conflict between Shias and Sunnis:

This is perhaps one of the biggest conflicts on planet Earth, and perhaps one of the easiest to resolve. It is astonishing that it has not been completely resolved so far, and in this respect, it shows the intelligence of the human being in extreme poor light.

A statistical analysis will show that the dispute between Shias and Sunnis is non-existent in Non-Muslim countries. It is also more or less non-existent in Muslim majority nations that are either predominantly Sunnis such as Saudi Arabia, or predominantly Shias such as Iran. The problem however, does exist significantly in Muslim majority nations where the ratio of Shia : Sunnis lies within 0.25 and 4.0. Take for example Iraq and Syria, where this dispute is rampant and is the root cause of the frequent civil wars in these two countries.

There is no doubt that there exists a massive divide between the various factions of Muslims (in particular the dispute between Sunnis and Shias, also known as Shiites). The divide began after the death of the prophet Mohammad. His followers could not agree on who was his successor. Those who considered the bloodline successor to be Ali (his cousin and son-in-law), were called Shiites, and those who chose Abu Bakr (his adviser) as the successor were called Sunnis. This divide is difficult to understand, considering the fact that centuries have passed since Mohammed's death, as well as the death of his successors. Why is there a need to choose a successor when Mohammad himself can be chosen, as he is the common denominator?

I ask the following questions: why do we need a successor? Do Buddhists want to know who Buddha's successor was? Do Christians want to know who Christ's successor was? Why is it important for Muslims to know who was chosen as Mohammed's successor?

There are enormously wide variations in the ideologies and beliefs of people in nearly every aspect of life, not just religion. Over the years, the split between factions widened appreciably, based on divisions due to different interpretations of the sacred texts, the role of mysticism, and whether the old tenets of faith should be updated or reformed. It is estimated that 80 percent of the world's Muslims are Sunnis, with large populations in Indonesia and other Asian countries, including Pakistan, Egypt, Turkey, Syria, and

Saudi Arabia in the Middle East. In Iraq and Iran, Shiites are the largest sect. Indian Muslims are of both types; they do not differentiate. Some Sunnis are zealously orthodox, such as the Wahhabis of Saudi Arabia. They interpret the Koran in a completely different way. The split between Sunnis and Shiites is getting more and more irrational with time. The Shiites of Iraq resented centuries of the Sunni rule while in Syria, the Shiites, who are in minority, rule the Sunni majority. The common people of both sects are no different from each other. It is only the leaders who exploit them for political ends, to obtain support for their own causes, regardless of whether they are good causes.

b. Religion Based Conflicts:

The parts of religious documents that relate to the intolerance of the so-called "nonbelievers", definitely need to be reformed.

I ask the following questions: Is there a nonbeliever? What does he or she look like? Is he or she wearing a t-shirt that reads, "I am a nonbeliever"? In essence, we cannot decide (or calculate) what we are, believers or nonbelievers, unless we can define what "God" is. What is the initial condition, or the definition of God based on which we can calculate and determine whether we are believers or not? Now, if we follow the dictionary meaning of God, which defines God as a "super human being" who controls nature, it turns out that we are all nonbelievers, for the simple reason that an anthropomorphic God (one who has physical function, one who is made up of atoms and molecules), cannot exist without violating the laws of science created by him.

On the other hand, if we define God as an "intelligent field" that controls nature, then we are all believers. However, it is to be understood that the quantum of intelligence or stupidity is a measure of the information in the field. Such an intelligent field, or God, is unlikely to come to our rescue if we are hell-bent on fighting wars. So, it turns out that we are all believers, and thus not in dispute with each other. No harm will be done if our religious documents are reformed to incorporate this truth.

c. Conflict between India and Pakistan:

In principle, there exists no conflict between the common people of the two countries. Hindus and Muslims have lived together for centuries; they look alike, they speak the same language, they sing the same songs, they watch the same movies, they have the same passion for cricket, I can go on and on.

There is no denying that the common people of the two countries would like to live in friendship and peaceful coexistence with each other. This is denied to them by the armies of the two nations, in particular, the Pakistan Army, and its belief that it is bound to lose its importance if there is peace with India, as well as its understanding that conflict through terrorism is more effective, not to mention substantially cheaper.

It is to be noted that if a war breaks out between the two countries, it will have to be fought under a nuclear overhang. There is no doubt whatsoever that the presence of nuclear weapons has substantially changed the way wars will be fought by these two nuclear adversaries.

d. Conflict between US, Russia and China

This is perhaps the most complex of them all. Even though I have covered it to a good extent in this book, it is still not enough. The Pugwash Group as well as the authors of Bulletin of Atomic Scientists have a significant role to play in educating the world leaders on the subject.

e. And so on, etc.

Leaders of nations must also be thoroughly well informed about several other issues that can lead to conflicts and wars which in turn can lead to nuclear wars.

Examples: Extreme Climate Changes, Bio Engineered Diseases, Perils of Artificial Intelligence, Uncontrolled Rise in Population, Corruption at High Places, Unfair Trade Practices, Selfish and Arrogant Nationalism etc.

TIME IS RUNNING OUT: IT IS TIME TO ACT

Once the concerned leaders of nation are thoroughly well equipped with knowledge and understanding, and are considered to possess a reasonably high value of the 'Compassion Index' as well as the 'Information Index', the dialogues and conferences should start. All participants in the dialogue process should understand the problems of the world from a neutral (global) perspective and not from the perspective of this or that religion.
(1A-14)
``The `PUGWASH` Group and the `BULLETIN OF ATOMIC SCIENTISTS` Group must play a very important role in facilitating THE
CONFERENCE.

Recall the Russel-Einstein Manifesto:

``*Most of us are not neutral in feeling, but as human beings, we have to remember, if the issues between the East and the West are to be decided in a manner that can satisfy everybody - whether a communist or an anti-communist, whether an Asian, European or American, whether white or black, then these issues must not be decided by war. We should wish this to be understood, both in the East and the West. Continuous progress in happiness, knowledge and wisdom lies before us, only if we choose it. Shall we instead choose death because we cannot forget our quarrels? We appeal as human beings to human beings: remember your humanity and forget the rest. If you can do so, the way to a new paradise lies open to you. If you cannot, there lies before you the risk of universal death*``.

The younger generation must rise to the occasion. If required, they must come to the streets in large numbers, to stage peace-rallies across the world.

Intelligence must conquer the Unintelligence.

This is not my book .. It is everyone`s book. The `Unity of Consciousness`, the `One-ness of the mind`, the Six Words .. `We all have the same mind`, the Equation of the Upanishads .. `Atman = Brahman`, the `Intelligent Field`, the `Travelling Cosmic Mind` etc etc .. imply that we are all one. But our consciousnesses are each in the singular, thus giving each one of us individual identities to play our parts in this Human-Drama. I request and urge the common people everywhere to get involved in whatever way they can to help in the continuation of the extraordinary intelligent life on this wonderful planet Earth.

With regard to the 9/11 attacks, every informed person is aware of the Deep State`s role in it.  Possibly, all living President`s of US know it. Most world leaders know it. Vladimir Putin knows it and is in possession of Satellite pictures in support. Structural Engineers and Architects of the world know it. Expert pilots of the world know it. Expert lawyers of the world know it. But it is still considered as an `Unpatriotic Conspiracy Theory` even though we cannot discredit the evidence that lies in the statement: ``Newton`s third law of motion cannot be violated``. Clearly, the evidence is compelling, and it can put the US Attorney in an unenviable position. It can also place the common man in America – particularly the sensitive type – in a terrible predicament, for he has to carry the stigma that he belongs to a nation whose leaders are engaged in stage managing unnecessary wars, and it makes it even worse for him when he realizes that he is paying for all this with his taxes.

With all this, it is unlikely that there will be further investigation into this sordid affair. It is best to forgive and forget .. and just consider it as an `aberration` of some kind. However, the least that should happen is the realization - significant awareness - that there is a Deep State in America, and in many other countries that must be taken care of.

On the question of what should be done about the Deep States of the world, one has to realize that the powerful industrial groups concerned in the manufacture of arms are doing their best in all countries to prevent the peaceful settlement of international disputes, and the rulers of some of these countries either do not mind this, or they do not have adequate control over their armies. But the people of these countries - particularly the younger generation – should understand this and vehemently yet peacefully voice their opinion against their leaders as well as against the leaders of their armies.. In this respect, the fate of nations hangs on the people themselves; each individual must always bear that in mind.

 Finally, the future security of the human race should not be left to the revolving doors of chance. It must be planned meticulously with no scope for miscalculations. Just as the Universe is a Designed Universe with immaculately designed constants of nature incorporated beautifully into the laws of science to enable life and consciousness to appear, and then understand the universe, in the same way actions of human beings (particularly of leaders of nations) should be meticulously designed to enable life and consciousness in the human form to continue forever – or at least for a billion years more, on planet Earth

In the words of Einstein:

``*May the conscience and the common sense of the peoples be awakened, so that we may reach a new stage in the life of nations, where people will look back on war as an incomprehensible aberration of their forefathers.* `` ``

---------   ---------   ---------

SWITCHED ON

I recently participated in a BBC Playwriting Competition for a Radio Play. My entry was a play in two acts titled 'SWITCHED ON.' The central idea of the play was the suggestion that our Universe is a simulated universe, and that it was a sort of super-consciousness that switched on the big bang of the current aeon of the universe. The primary hook in the story is the realisation that 'Simulation' is the preferred choice over 'Randomness.' A 'Simulation' is necessary so that, as far as possible, everything happens in accordance with plans and designs to yield the desired results. In the case of the Universe as a whole, the desired result is that life and consciousness should exist and flourish in various parts. In the case of the human civilization, the desired results are peaceful coexistence, avoidance of conflicts and wars, with compassionate, able, and responsible leaders at the helm of every country. 'Randomness' should have little chance of coming in the way of these desired results.

All in all, it is to be ensured that men with an inadequate Compassion and Information Index, should have zero chances of becoming Presidents of Nations.

Chapter Five

'Switched On' .. Arguments For And Against A Simulated Universe

EXTRACTS FROM A CONVERSATION:

The conversation took place between commenters in response to a blog "Can Black Holes Tell Us Something About Digital Computers?" This was posted on the Huffington Post on 1st August 2013, by the Scientist Mario Livio. Two of these characters are 'Charlie Fox Trot' and 'Diogenes of Alaska'. These were pseudonyms of course, as their actual names are not known to me. The third character was Surendra Kumar Sagar (yours truly), who wrote a major response to the blog, suggesting that our universe is a simulated one, and that it was a kind of super-consciousness that switched on the big bang of the current aeon of the universe.

My response triggered a very lengthy and hugely interesting conversation between the three of us. Charlie strongly opposed my idea of 'A Simulated Universe' and gave ample justification of why he thought I was wrong. Though Diogenes of Alaska did not oppose my idea, he however wanted me to have a pragmatic approach on the subject and not be carried away by such speculative ideas, unless I had a reasonably firm grip on the totality of propositions entailed by what I put forward.

Given below is an extract from that conversation *(5A-01):*

Charlie Fox Trot: I must caution you SK, that just because the universe has many symmetries, it does not give rise to the notion that the universe is in fact a simulation.

SK: The universe has many constants - extremely fine-tuned, embedded into the laws of the universe - that caused theoretical physicists to arrive and then understand the universe, which gives rise to the notion that the universe is in fact a simulation. Many such mathematical constants were required to be fixed and incorporated in the programme, by a certain 'Something' (such as probably a super-consciousness), to ensure that life and consciousness should emerge sometime and understand the universe. Surely the universe would not perform such a stunning show as the 'Big Bang' to empty stalls.

We are the 'Audience' that 'Something' contemplated. But I don't believe that 'Something' was 'Someone.' I call it the 'INTELLIGENT FIELD.'

CFT: The idea that the universe is a 'simulation', is not even scientifically coherent. Let us say that fine tuning of natural laws is proof that a universe with these laws is a simulation. The universe in which our universe is being simulated must be at least as mathematically powerful as the universe we reside in; otherwise a simulation of our universe would not be possible. There are vastly more conceivable worlds that are less mathematically powerful than ours. Therefore, any world which can simulate our world must also be fine-tuned. Now, if the world that simulates our world is fine-tuned, then that is proof that it is ALSO a simulation. Therefore, there is a third world which is simulating this one. By the above logic, that world must be simulated, and so on.

Therefore, by your logic SK, no universe is non-simulated. There is no meaningful distinction between a simulated and a non-simulated universe. In fact, a sufficiently powerful simulation is mathematically identical to the 'real' thing, so the idea of a simulated, as opposed to non-simulated, universe is entirely incoherent.

Diogenes of Alaska: It's not that simple, Charlie. If it were that simple, it would be easy to rule out the Cantor set. Besides, whether something is coherent, does NOT depend on whether it is 'scientifically' coherent. On the contrary, it is the job of science, expertise and education to ensure that at the very least 'coherence' is not a property that needs to be judged by experts. And given the Cantor set, that is certainly not easy. The difference between pathological and non-pathological arguments should not itself be subject to debate.

CFT: We can rule out the Cantor set as an object in a physically realisable Universe. But that's beside the point. My argument was using reductio ad absurdum on the SPECIFIC argument used by SK, that fine tuning of laws somehow represented evidence of a PHYSICAL simulation of our universe in another universe. There's a whole host of other, thornier philosophical arguments to be had about simulations in general. I don't think the idea of our universe being a simulation is coherent, but I should have phrased it better to avoid making it seem as if that was the intention of my argument, when the argument was merely that fine-tuned laws was evidence that the universe was physically simulated in another universe is incoherent.

SK: Here we are talking 'philosophy.' Neither can I say with 100% certainty that the universe is a simulation, nor can anyone say with 100% certainty that it is not.

This universe though 13.7 billion years old, is still considered to be in its infancy. The degrees of consciousness and the levels of intelligence are forever increasing, and there will be ample time to know the truth regarding 'simulation'.

For the time being, let us consider the evidence available and then judge ourselves what is the probability that the universe could in fact have been 'simulated'.

When we do that, when we study the evidences available, when we look at these constants, when we see how extremely fine-tuned they are in such an extremely narrow range - and there are so many of them - each one of them has to be that finely tuned for the desired end results. We will realise that the probability of the universe not being a 'simulated' one is just about as low - as I said before - as that of an aircraft getting assembled by a tornado striking a junkyard.

CFT: That's not a good argument SK. All teleological arguments about the nature of the universe are no good. The fine-tuning argument that you are using, makes the assumptions that:

a. Natural Constants are 100% arbitrary (i.e. they could just as well have been of any value, with intrinsic changes to our physics).
b. Life of ANY KIND must be like ours and can only exist in 'possible' worlds very close to ours.
c. There is only one universe and it is this exact one we are in.

First, you blow (c) out of the water by making this an argument about simulation. If there is another universe where we are being simulated, then maybe there are infinite numbers of universes with slightly different laws. You have no reason to pick 'simulation' over 'unguided anthropic selection.' It is a matter of choice. What we know is perfectly consistent with a multiverse, generally inhospitable to life.

When it comes to (b), there is surely an infinite variety of information processing species possible in all of these infinite 'possible' worlds, according to their physics. Basing your argument on the necessity of carbon-based Earth life is not good logic.

In (a), we have no reason to assume the natural constants you think are 'fine-tuned' to be arbitrary. For all we know they can be established mathematically from fundamental principles. Choosing to believe that they are arbitrary is again a choice, but a totally unscientific one.

151

SK: Maybe the required quantum of simulation is not that high. It is not that each and every activity is a consequence of that simulation. Perhaps it is a notional simulation of some kind. Only a computer programme was prepared and the mathematical constants provided as inputs by the designers. But the designers had no control over 'randomness', 'probability' and the 'laws of causation.'

The designers could not say when and where life would emerge to understand the universe, or when a civilization from planet 'x' would conquer a civilization from planet 'y', or if Obama would win a certain election. One just switches on a button and then sees what happens.

This also explains all the imperfections in our world.

It is like when we press a button to cause a massive explosion in a crowded city. We are sure the damage will be done, but we cannot say which buildings will be destroyed or precisely how many people will be killed.

CFT: The 'imperfections' of the world are a well-understood result of chaotic dependence on initial conditions and thermodynamic entropy. They don't need a metaphysical explanation beyond that.

As for your point of view, 'it is not that each and every activity is a consequence of that simulation. Only a computer programme was prepared and the mathematical constants provided as inputs by the designers.' The problem is that you need some computational substrate for this simulation to exist in, so in fact, every activity HAS to be a consequence of that simulation. What I mean is you can't just say (to be flip) 'let there be light' and have a simulation of light appear; you have to have a system that can simulate it. That's what a simulation IS. The point I'm making is that YOU seem to be implying that the simulation is a mechanism being controlled by designers. My argument is that the computational substrate could as easily be an abstract simulation in the realm of platonic forms.

All simulations of our universe would be equivalent mathematically, so there is no need to assume more than necessary; like there are intelligent designers behind its creation.

SK: Charlie Fox Trot (I like the name), with regard to your argument 'the mere fact that there are those fine-tuned constants embedded in nature, is no evidence that the universe was physically simulated by someone in another universe', this indeed is a valid point. Here again, we are talking philosophy, rather deep 'philosophy'. Neither can I say with 100% certainty that the 'simulation' was actually a 'physical simulation' carried out by the super-consciousness of the pre big bang universe, nor can anyone say with 100 % certainty that the 'simulation' happened on its own, i.e. by 'Magic' or 'An act of God' or something.

Both alternatives require 'carrying a quantum of metaphysical baggage'.Here, I think it can be said that in the former case i.e. 'Super consciousness doing the trick', it's a finite quantum of metaphysical baggage that needs to be carried. Whereas in the latter case i.e. 'Magic doing the trick (An act of God)', it looks like this quantum is enormously high - perhaps infinite.

CFT: It is a rather deep philosophy. I tend to side with Plato on this subject, specifically that the universe we live in is a partial representation of a perfect mathematical reality. Some might look at this and call it 'simulation', and that phrase has been used an awful lot in Plato's presence.

However, my major point is that there is a huge difference between the Platonic simulation (matter simulating form) and computational simulation (form simulating matter). This is what most people are talking about when they argue that the world is simulated.

Both have some concept they are modeling and some substrate they are using to model it with. Plato's forms are pure mathematical ideas, and the substrate is essentially matter. Matter acts as the computer and forms the software. A computational simulation (like the ancestor simulations some trans-humanists talk about), has a pre-existing idea of reality as its model, and some kind of computer as its substrate.

The huge difference here is that in platonic simulation, our physical reality is a byproduct of the simulation of forms. In computational simulation, physical reality is the intended end-product, which brings into question where the physical reality being modeled comes from, and leads to infinite regress.

DOA to CFT: Charlie, the argument in favour of our universe being a simulation is a different one. Its core goes like this, and it is perfectly plausible - as far as it goes:

"A long-proposed and thought experiment, put forward by both philosophers and popular culture, points out that any civilization of sufficient size and intelligence would eventually create a simulated universe if such a thing were possible. And since there would therefore be many more simulations (within simulations) than real universes, it is therefore more likely than not that our world is artificial."

It is merely a challenge. Food for thought. But it is also good enough to debunk the entirety of New Atheism in one paragraph.

I am so sad that I didn't come up with that paragraph. But at least I'm not denying it.

If you just take this idea and ask yourself, what would happen to folks living 5000 years ago when they came across something like it? What would they do?

Prove that the Continuum Hypothesis is independent from the remaining axioms of Zermelo Fraenkel set theory? Or come up with a religious myth of the creation of the world by a superior intelligence?

And most importantly, which one of the two has better chances to survive for the number of millennia it takes, so that somebody can tackle the foundations of mathematics; telling us that the answer is approximately 42.

CFT: Uh huh Diogenes, you are talking about ancestor simulations; but with Surendra, I was responding to using a fine-tuning argument, so that is what I focused on.

The problem with this idea is that we have very good reason to think that it is NOT possible to create such a simulation, except on a limited scale. That is to say that fundamental limitations (in our case the Bekenstein bound, that limits the amount of information that can exist in a volume of space, and thermodynamic considerations, not to mention the economic impracticality of such an endeavor), would force our simulation to be limited compared to our universe, or in other words, a simulation of the universe utilising all the space and energy of that universe, would be that universe, and not a simulation.

Therefore, because all simulations are small, and nested ones even smaller, the original universe would be staggeringly large and contain the vast majority of people. This, I think, totally invalidates that argument.

DOA: So you rely on the strong Leibniz Principle and a rough estimate on sizes of abstractly possible universes, in order to settle a metaphysical dispute that is at least as undecidable as the fine structure of the Cantor set.

Some people are really brave around here.

As for your remark on SK's argument, 'All teleological arguments about the nature of the universe are stupid.'

155

That's a pretty strong claim given that the best theories about the nature of the universe are so far unable to reconcile the very small and the very big. Under those circumstances, who is to rule out the possibility that the only way to 'round up' our understanding may even require teleology? Or something similar, like 'entelechy'?

Because you don't like theology and metaphysics? Is that the reason why? Then please explain to me the non-metaphysical documentation of this:

"We have no reason to assume the natural constants you think are 'fine tuned' to be arbitrary. For all we know they can be established mathematically from fundamental principles. Choosing to believe that they are arbitrary is again, a choice, and a totally unscientific one."

First of all, 'we' clearly cannot establish mathematically from fundamental principles, constants of the Standard Model. But even assuming that 'we' could, how would that be non-metaphysical and non-theological?

For all I can tell, you have NO way of ruling out that the answer will prove equivalent to some variant of 'entelechy'. In fact, the only alternative seems to admit that theory will arrive at the limit of its wits. Or has already done so.

CFT: "How would that be non-metaphysical and non-theological?"

You are using a straw man here. There's nothing inherently theological about mathematics.

As for metaphysics, when you are talking about the mathematical underpinnings of nature, you are talking about something INHERENTLY metaphysical. I'm not sure what your issue is here.

Teleological arguments are not good evidence of intelligent design. You can only ascribe them to intelligence when you have either;

a. Given some other persuasive evidence that intelligence could exist - we have no evidence either way at this point.
b. Proven that no other argument suffices to explain the phenomenon.

In either case, you need much more persuasive arguments to support the teleological one. As for unguided teleology - like the strong anthropic principle - you still need evidence of some unguided mechanism which can be selected for the desired outcome. Your argument may be true, but it needs a lot of evidence.

Simply from the basis of logic, teleology should be avoided in science, unless absolutely necessary. You are right that it may be true, but it is probably not.

As for establishing constants from first principles, we have done that already with some constants. Pi, for example, began as an observed phenomenon; every time we measured circles we got the same answer. But the value of Pi arises essentially from the nature of Euclidean space; it couldn't be any other value. That is the kind of thing I suspect we will find about the 'fine-tuned' constants.

DOA: It is very refreshing that you are not worried about metaphysics at all. Very rare too in these forums. You clearly don't seem to be a materialist either. We can quickly agree that indeed there is something inherently metaphysical about the role of mathematics in all sufficiently rich models of nature.

Whether that makes mathematics theological or not is another question. There are guesses and opinions though. For example, a famous Bourbakist once said, "We know that god must exist

157

because mathematics is consistent, and we know that the devil must exist because we cannot prove it."

I didn't defend Intelligent Design (in the sense of the movement) and never will. Teleology and even 'Creationism' is something else. What I claim is that you can't prove them inconsistent, not with the means you need to assume when you believe in a unified theory of the universe, and not without those means. Hence, never, no matter what.

Your optimism with respect to the mathematical meaning of the constants of the Standard Model is breath-taking, and on certain days I would like to share that optimism.

But then I watched the movie "Pi" and recalled that numerology isn't science.

DOA TO SK: Surendra, you are making very interesting points, but trying to answer too many things at once invariably leads to a lack of precision. Ultimately, the assumption that there must be a way of making all of this stuff clear, may not be warranted. I agree that we cannot rule out the idealist view that traces everything back to consciousness. But historically, such attempts have always resulted in worldviews that lacked in resilience.

Scientism is merely the other extreme and doesn't work either. But the core problem is the lack of resilience. To avoid that problem, help only comes from pragmatism. And that means, among other things, accepting that we may not be able to figure it all out. Nor do we need to.

SK TO DOA: I already said that we may not be able to figure it all out for a long long time. But as the degrees of consciousnesses and levels of intelligence keep increasing with time, we will keep getting closer and closer to that - the figuring it all out stage.

On "Nor do we need to."

Do we need to play football, watch movies, eat out etc.? We do it as we find it interesting.

Besides, philosophical discussions (not limited to the 'simulation' issue), will forever remain a continuous process; in the broadest sense (or nonsense), there are only two players playing this game of 'Reality' and their names are:

1. 'Matter and Energy' hereafter denoted by the symbol 'MAE'.
2. 'Mind and Consciousness' we call it 'MAC'.

We do not know who came first, but it looks like MAC is the primary player and has complete control over MAE.

MAC, on reaching a state of super consciousness, prepares a comprehensive programme with beautifully designed mathematical constants. It then switches on the computer at the appropriate time, and ushers in the next big bang; after trillions of years the next, and so on. A cyclic phenomenon. We could call MAC as Mathematics who gives orders, and call MAE as Physics who follows these orders.

Indeed 'Mathematics' is the President and the company is called 'The Universe.'

DOA: Alright. I see. Pretty cool.

I was just a little worried that maybe you weren't aware of the fact that speculative thought needs some constraints too.

Although I'm not entirely sure what exactly it would mean to 'agree' with your point of view, I'm basically open to it. It might be the truth. But as I said, most of the time I prefer to act and think in contexts where it's just a little bit easier to tell whether or not I have a firm grip on the totality of propositions entailed.

SK: Thanks DOA. Yes, I am aware that speculative thought needs some constraints, and the biggest constraint is that the truth already established by Science must not be violated, and I am trying my best to follow this principle.

CFT indeed has some valid objections to 'Physical simulation by intelligent designers', such as:

1. Some computational substrate is required for the 'simulation' to exist in, and that this computational substrate could as easily be an abstract simulation in the realm of platonic forms.
2. It is not possible to create a 'simulation' except on a limited scale. A simulation of the universe utilising all the space and energy of that universe would BE that universe, and not a simulation.

At the current level of knowledge, it is difficult to give a satisfactory reply to counter these objections without recourse to some metaphysics or 'Teleology'. Your views on 'teleology/entelechy' too are very interesting and insightful.

But then the current level of knowledge is indeed insignificant compared to what it would be a few thousand years from now.

In about some hundred thousand years, we have become men from apes. It is reasonable to assume that after a similar time gap or even less, we would become 'super minds' and then these problems of understanding 'simulation' would not be insurmountable, and what looks like teleology would be well explained by Science.

There can be several possible scenarios of 'Physical Simulations'. A large scale (full universe level) 'simulation', carried out by the ultimate 'super-consciousness' is a possibility that in no case can be ruled out. Erwin Schrodinger's (and Charles Sherrington's) concept of the 'Oneness of mind' together with a distinct possibility of the intelligent mind's omnipresence, can lead towards the

160

hypothesis of a super conscious designer doing the 'simulation'. Perhaps it may not be 'nonsense' to consider 'Intelligence' to be a compound. How can we, with our limited knowledge, deny this?

Perhaps the 'Omnipresent mind' or 'something' could also explain 'quantum entanglement', not to mention 'collapse of the wave function'.Or perhaps, I am out of my mind.

DOA: Refer to 'Objections to physical simulations.'

Let me admit that I don't believe at all in physical simulations of universes, and I don't think I ever claimed anything else. Also, I don't believe in extrapolating future knowledge or possible future knowledge. The use of the thought experiment is that it elucidates aspects of our own evolution of understanding. I don't think it can help us find out something new about the world.

Sometimes it can be ok to violate 'truths already established by science'.But usually this requires the use of means that are extremely difficult to keep under control. The reason why some 'truths already established by science' may turn out to be false, is because those who established them were already in the same situation, and didn't control enough of the consequences of their new approach; but nobody found out so far.

It has been like that for quite a while now. And to get beyond that dance (which is probably impossible), may require teleology or entelechy. But it is also possible that humans cannot include that mode of thought within a scientific worldview.

This means that pragmatism may always remain one step ahead of theory. Why sacrifice the openness of the scientific process for the sake of the appearance of a more comprehensive theory? The price is that the scientific worldview remains incomplete. But that is not a problem, as long as we don't expect from a scientific worldview what religion and philosophy promised but couldn't deliver.

As I said, we cannot rule out these scenarios (or some version of them). But that doesn't mean we can support them with evidence. It still means that they can be made with some consistency; it means it is not surprising that people have come up with the notion and concept of a transcendent mind. There is nothing in these thoughts that violates science, or at least there is a way of rendering these thoughts that doesn't violate science.

END OF CONVERSATION

Notwithstanding the fact that at the current level of our understanding, it is impossible to establish the number of aeons that preceded the current aeon of the universe, and the manner in which simulation took place and under what mechanism could the constants of nature have been implanted in the system that 'Switched On' the big bang, the fact remains that the operation was hugely successful in creating an eternal and everlasting universe with life and consciousness evolving and flourishing in the galaxies.

All that is required now is to establish how the universe can make sense, and what can be that philosophical model that ensures permanent consciousness for us all.

Chapter Six
The Standard Model Of Philosophy

"Whatever their differences of opinion about the nature of God, I know of no religion that does not teach that God is a mind." Paul Davies

A Standard Model - such as that of 'Particle Physics' or 'Cosmology' - in general, signifies a model which has been developed, as far as possible, based on the established principles of science.

In which case, you might ask the question: How is the said term 'Standard Model' used for philosophy? For philosophy is after all philosophy. If it were an established truth, it wouldn't be called philosophy.

In fact, what exactly is the meaning of the word 'Philosophy'?

Let me use some high school algebra to understand this.

If 'x' corresponds to the total ultimate truth and 'y' corresponds to a portion of truth that is fully understood and established by science, then 'z'=x-y obviously corresponds to that portion of the truth which is either unknown or partly known and not yet established by science.

The entire philosophy of the world - whether written in books/websites or discussed in seminars/get-togethers or in 'Talks' like this - is dealing with 'z'. The portion of it that is related to topics such as 'mind', 'consciousness', 'soul', 'spirit', and 'God' is dealing with 'Religious Philosophy'. As and when a portion of 'z' becomes an established truth by science (experiment/observation), it gets added to 'y'. Until such time, it remains in the domain of philosophy/religion.

So what should this 'Standard Model of Philosophy' aim at?

Simple. The universe must make sense.

THE UNIVERSE MUST MAKE SENSE

The laws of science must be such that the 'universe should make sense', and for the universe to make sense, there must be a consciousness to observe and to understand that the universe makes sense.

But is our universe obliged to make sense?

In other words, 'is making sense a requirement that the universe must fulfil?'

Somehow it looks like scientists are not too interested in answering this question. There are some, and that includes some great scientists, who believe that the universe is under no obligation to make sense. According to them, what we know about the universe is perfectly consistent with a multiverse generally inhospitable to life. As for me, I am NOT a member of this club of scientists.

Scientists will someday have a complete understanding of what dark matter is; what dark energy is. Scientists will someday have a theory that explains everything about matter and energy. But can that theory be called a 'Theory of Everything'; can we say that will be the end of physics?

I don't think so.

Any TOE that does not take into account Mind and Consciousness, along with its impact on Matter and Energy, is incomplete. Any TOE that does not explain what caused the big bang is incomplete.

It is not enough to proceed with the assumption that the big bang happened at time zero. Trying to understand what caused the Big Bang may be in the domain of philosophy, but whenever it is understood, it will have to be considered physics.

It is possible that after trillions of years, dark energy will drive the universe via accelerated expansion, towards perpetual nothingness, to wipe the slate clean. But that won't be the end of everything. Rather it must be considered as a platform for resetting conditions in preparation for the next cycle.

Any theory that does not guarantee a continuity of a universe with life and consciousness is incomplete. In fact, this aspect must be set as a precondition for arriving at any meaningful TOE. Any theory that leads towards a future of perpetual nothingness and ends there, is unacceptable to the thinking mind.

But there are complexities here that must be resolved. Even the greatest scientists differed on conclusions even though the inputs available to them were similar. Einstein was in perennial disagreement with Niels Bohr on the 'Completeness/Incompleteness of Quantum Mechanics' issue *(6A-01)*. John Wheeler and Wigner were involved in a major argument on 'What Happens Inside A Black Hole' during the 1979 Centennial symposium to celebrate the achievements of Einstein *(6A-02)*. Stephen Hawking disagreed with Roger Penrose on 'Objective Reduction Of The Wave Function And Its Role In The Operation Of The Brain' on the necessity to explain consciousness *(6A-03)*.

But we can squeeze the complexities and arrive at certain simple statements that do not contradict established truths, and are in the domain of possibilities.

In the words of John Wheeler:

"In time to come, a single simple sentence will explain the strangeness of the universe and as we say that sentence to each other we'll say - Oh how beautiful - how could we have missed it all that time?"

One such candidate for a single simple sentence is this: "WE ALL HAVE THE SAME MIND" *(6A-04)*
It's just that our consciousness is in the singular.

It is a 'Travelling Cosmic Mind' that gives us everlasting consciousness. An 'Intelligent Field' that is always on the lookout for creating an appropriate biochemistry to give itself consciousness and then understand itself and the universe, allows the universe to make sense.

We ask the question: Why 'Travelling'? Is this 'Intelligent Field' not omnipresent in Time and Space as is the 'Electromagnetic Field' and the 'Gravitational Field'?

To answer this question, we need to understand the future of the universe. As per the existing theories of the universe, notwithstanding the fact that they might still be in the domain of philosophy, there is a reasonable consensus of opinion that there are five distinct stages in the life of the universe; in each of which the universe looks completely different.

To begin with, the universe has a long life, in excess of 10^{100} years i.e. more than ten thousand trillion trillion trillion trillion trillion trillion trillion trillion years, and the five distinct eras of the universe are as follows:

The first period is called the 'PREMORDIAL ERA' which lasts for about three hundred thousand years. No stars, no galaxies. Nothing but radiation. No atoms formed and extremely high temperatures that are reducing all the time.

The second period is called the 'STELLIFEROUS ERA' which begins as the Primordial Era ends, and lasts for about a thousand trillion years i.e. about 10^15 years.

We are currently living in this era and the current age of the universe is about 13.7 billion years, which is less than 1 in 70000 parts of even the Stelliferrous Era. So, the universe is currently just an infant, or maybe a new born baby. What happens in the Stelliferrous Era? Galaxies are getting formed, stars are shinning, life and consciousness is flourishing. Liquid water is available and carbon-based life is possible at many locations (star systems with planets) in this period.

The third period is called the 'DEGENERATE ERA'. Stars stop shining and start dying. The dead stellar remnants such as Brown Dwarfs, White Dwarfs, Neutron Stars and Black Holes constitute the inventory of this era. This period lasts until about 10^40 years (since the big bang).

About a hundred trillion years might be a common overlapping period between the two eras. Many of these dead stars collide with each other; scatter into space and into nothingness. Of these, only the outer atmospheres of large White Dwarfs that can support interesting chemical actions, are possible candidates for supporting some sort of the abstract life. The energy source could be the radiation field heating from within, though carbon, oxygen and many other elements required for supporting life will be available. Liquid water will be missing, and that is why the nature of life will be quite different from what it is on earth.

The fourth period is called the 'BLACKHOLE ERA'. This lasts for about a trillion trillion trillion trillion trillion trillion years, going all the way to 10^100 years, since the big bang. Black Holes inherit the universe, warp space and time, evaporate their mass energy, and make an explosive exit.

Life is extremely difficult in this longest lasting of the four Eras, unless life is of a highly abstract nature, with actual matter not taking any part in the proceedings. According to Freeman Dyson, the metabolic rate of an abstract creature is proportional to its operating temperature, and so is the rate of consciousness. The largest temperature accessible at black hole surfaces is about a billion times smaller than the operating temperature of a human being. Accordingly, the rate of consciousness is slower by a factor of several billion.

The final era is called the 'DARK ERA'. It goes beyond 10^{100} years, looks like a never ending, nothing-going-on-here era except for photons moving here and there. *(6A-05)*

We ask the question: For how long can we expect life and consciousness to exist with a reasonably high rate and degree of consciousness?

A reasonable estimate is 10^{15} years, i.e. up to the end of the Stelliferrous Era. However, even if we consider an overlapping period lasting about a thousand times longer than the Stelliferrous Era into the degenerate era (which is highly improbable), the most optimistic estimate is worked out as 10^{18} years since the big bang.

Now compare this with the least optimistic estimate of the life of the universe at 10^{100} years, i.e. completely ignoring the Dark Era of the deepest future.

What do we get?

We get life and consciousness flourishing at a good rate, and the degree of consciousness that lasts for only one unit of time out of nearly 10^{82} units of time.

Does this make sense at all?

Or can we say that making sense is not a requirement that the universe must fulfill?

But we are conscious. We have always been conscious (even if there were intervening periods of unconsciousness, we were unconscious of these unconsciousness tenures, so they passed quickly). Indeed, we are forever conscious for we do not remember ever asking the question, 'Where is the universe for me?'

In short it cannot be that the universe does not make sense.

How does the 'Intelligent Field' resolve this dilemma?

I can only speculate with a wild imagination, but there is a good chance I may be right, for that is the only way out. This mind of ours is nothing but a 'TRAVELLING COSMIC MIND.'

To remain forever conscious, the only requirement is that we remain forever in the Stelliferrous Era, where stars are shining, life and consciousness is flourishing. The only way this can happen is if we consider our 'mind' to be integral with a cosmic mind that can travel backwards and forwards in time, and thus remain forever in the Stelliferrous Era. In short, if our mind is an omnipresent 'Infinite mind' - omnipresent not just in space but also in time.

The mind does not travel into the deep future, for the simple reason that it cannot obtain consciousness there.

But is that possible?

I should say it is distinctly possible, in fact, it is impossible to be impossible.
No doubt of course, that the concept of the traveling cosmic mind is a challenging one; it is very difficult to prove, but I guess, even more difficult to disprove. It has several positives such as the following:

1. It does not violate any of the established principles of science. On May 31st 2016, I gave a talk on the subject of the traveling cosmic mind at the prestigious National Institute of Advanced Studies in Bangalore. It was attended by several eminent scientists and philosophers of Bangalore. No doubts were raised on the idea during the question and answer period. In general, it was well received.

2. It dispenses with the requirement of a multiverse theory, which requires the existence of millions of universes, so that at least one universe has absolutely the precise mathematical constants of nature (as in this universe), so that life and consciousness will appear and then understand the universe. One universe, with all its aeons, is all that is required for the cosmic mind to travel back and forth in time to remain forever in the Stelliferrous Era; to obtain consciousness and to not proceed toward the Degenerate, Black Hole and Dark Eras of the deep future, where no consciousness is available.

3. It does not require the big bang to be in the time zero (i.e. the beginning) of the universe as an act of God. It assumes the requirement of a long history of several previous aeons of the universe, leading in the end to a primordial consciousness, just ontologically prior to the physical realities of the current aeon of the universe that contained the coded information for constructing a possible new universe. That coded information constitutes the design of the new universe, complete with all the fine-tuned mathematical constants built into the program.

4. It is in complete agreement with the concept of 'Oneness of the Mind.' It is just that our consciousness is in the singular; it is the traveling cosmic mind that gives us everlasting consciousness. An 'Intelligent Field', which is forever and always on the lookout for creating an appropriate biochemistry to give itself consciousness, thus allows the universe to make sense.

5. It gives a meaning to the universe. Without the traveling cosmic mind, the universe would be completely meaningless; life and consciousness would exist for only one unit of time (the Stelliferrous Era) out of nearly 1082 units of time, as explained earlier.

6. It is in complete consonance with Einstein's Relativity Principle (ERP), and adequately takes care of explaining all the various 'causality violation paradoxes', that ensue as a consequence of ERP.

7. It is strong and intelligent. It will keep producing islands of negative entropy for life and consciousness to flourish and understand the universe, not just for a while, but for all times to come. Without it, the arrow of time will always point to the dissolution of structure into a featureless state of maximum entropy. Indeed, the traveling cosmic mind comes to our rescue and saves us from that bleak future.

8. It explains the concept of quantum entanglement perfectly. The mere fact that there is such a thing as quantum entanglement implies instant connectivity, and this connectivity is impossible to imagine except by the consideration of an omnipresent mind (omnipresent in time as well as space).

Now some people are advising me to be more pragmatic in my approach, and not be too excited about the traveling cosmic mind (particularly the traveling part). Some have said that all these ideas will remain unverifiable until our present limited consciousness evolves ultimately into an infinite mind (IM). However, all have agreed with the idea that mind and consciousness have a central place in the ultimate nature of reality. Notwithstanding the power of the traveling cosmic mind in its capacity to give us everlasting consciousness and awareness, the same is powerless, when it is a question of exercising control over the consciousness; when it becomes a part of a living organism, even if that living organism is a human body.

As I wrote earlier, while there is an intelligent field in control, the amount of intelligence in that intelligent field is a measure of the information in the field. The current information reveals that the intelligent field is severely contaminated. The present crop of world leaders is unable to deal with the contamination; some are even causing it.

Time is running out for us if we are to save the human race from extinction. The cosmic mind will not come to our rescue, and the beautiful minds of the world must come forward with novel and intelligent ideas that can save us from the perils faced by our species. Leaders of nations must come forward to implement them. Once there was a Manhattan Project, which saved the planet from the very real danger of a fascist world. Now, a new Manhattan Project is required to explore other forms of power and paths to peace.

In the end, I repeat these words:

"Avoidance of extinction must be the most important subject taught in universities worldwide."

NOTES AND REFERENCES

1A-01   For further reading and many more Churchill quotations refer to 'Churchill's BOMB' by Graham Farmelo. Faber & Faber (2013)

1A-01A   Extracts from the book 'Lise Meitner: A Life in Physics by Ruth Lewin Sime'. University of California Press (1976) Pages 236-237

1A-02   Extract from the book 'Einstein: The Life and Times by Ronald W. Clarke'. Avon Books (1971,1984) Page 681

1A-03   For further reading, refer to "Some Strangeness in the Proportion" (a chapter in 'Albert Einstein: Encounter with America', edited by Harry Woolf). Addison Wesley Publishing Company Inc. Massachusetts (1980)

1A-04   For a comprehensive account of the dropping of the bombs, I selected some extracts from the book 'The Manhattan Project' (edited by Cynthia C. Kelley), which is a ground-breaking collection of essays, articles, documents, and excerpts from histories, biographies, plays, novels, and letters on the subject. Black Dog and Leventhal Publisher (2007) Passages selected from the section on 'Dropping the Bombs' Page 317 onwards.

1A–04A: Also, from 'The Manhattan Project', passages selected from the section 'Living with the Bomb' – A Cold War Warning – The Russel Einstein Manifesto Pages 444 - 447

1A-05   For further reading, refer to 'Keeper of the Nuclear Conscience' by Andrew Brown Oxford University Press (2012) refer also to my review of this book on www.aAmazon.com.

1A-06   Extract from the book 'The Meaning of the 21st Century A Vital Blueprint for Ensuring Our Future' by James Martin. Riverhead Trade NYC 2007 (First published 2006)

1A-07   Extracts from 'Keeper of the Nuclear Conscience' by Andrew Brown.

1A-07A   Refer article: "A posthumous honor for the man who saved the world" by Max Tegmark Analysis Nuclear Risk, Nuclear Weapons (Bulletin of Atomic Scientists)

1A-08:   This is best described in an extract from the article "Engaging India: Diplomacy, Democracy, and the Bomb," by Strobe Talbot (taken from Google).

1A-09   M. S. Swaminathan, the former president of the Pugwash conferences, and Charles Townes, famous scientist and inventor of the laser, were among the speakers at the 2003 symposium, "Science and Beyond," held at the National Institute of Advanced Studies, Bangalore. My wife and I were among the delegates at the symposium.

1A-10   Extract from the book 'Ideas and Opinions' by Albert Einstein. Roopa and Company Calcutta (13th Impression 1996)

1A-11   Extract from the book 'What We Say Goes' by Noam Chomsky. Penguin Books (2009).

1A-12   Extract from V. R. Raghavan's review of the book 'India's Sentinel', which is about Air Commodore Jasjit Singh's select writings on the subject.

1A-13   Extract from a blog on investmentwatchblog.com by Mike Adams. It is not clear to what extent the information content in this extract is reliable and authentic; nevertheless, it gives a reasonable indication of the current mind-set of the leaders of the three great nations, the United States, Russia, and China.

1A-14   Added in the second edition.

3A-01   Quote from the book 'Information and the Nature of Reality (IATNOR)', edited by Paul Davies and Niels Henrik Gregerson. Cambridge University Press (2011) from the essay "What Is Missing from Theories of Information?" by Terrence W Deacon.

3A-02   Quote from 'IATNOR'. From the essay "The Computational Universe" by Seth Lloyd.

3A-03   Quote from 'IATNOR'. From the essay "Semiotic Freedom: An Emerging Force" by Jesper Hoffmeyer.

3A-04   Quote from 'IATNOR'. From the essay "God as the Ultimate Informational Principle" by Keith Ward.

3A-05   Quote from 'IATNOR'. From the essay "Unsolved Dilemmas: The Concept of Matter in the History of Philosophy and Contemporary Physics" by Philip Clayton.

3A-06   Quote from 'IATNOR'. From the essay "Universe from Bits" by Paul Davies.

3A-07   Quote from 'IATNOR'. From the essay "Minds and Values in the Quantum Universe" by Henry Stapp.

3A-08   Quote from 'Emperor's New Mind' by Roger Penrose

3A-09   Quote from 'IATNOR'. From the essay "What Is the Spiritual Body?" by Michael Welker.

3A- 10   Quote from the book 'The New Quantum Age' by Andrew Whitaker. Oxford University Press (2012)

5A-01   For the full conversation between commenters in response to the blog "Can Black Holes Tell Us Something About Digital Computers?" by the Scientist Mario Livio, refer the author's website 'www.sixwords.in' under 'Interactions'.

6A-01   Refer 'Einstein Bohr and the Quantum Dilemma' by Andrew Whitaker, Cambridge University Press (1996).

6A-02   Refer 'Some Strangeness In The Proportion' Edited by Harry Woolf, Addison Wesley Publishing Company Inc. Massachusetts (1980).

6A-03   Refer 'The Large, The Small, And The Human Mind' by Roger Penrose, Cambridge University Press (1994).

6A-04   These are the Six Words of 'SIX WORDS' by Surendra
         Kumar Sagar, Create Space Independent Publishing
         Platform (2014)
6A-05   Refer 'Intelligent Field' by Surendra Kumar Sagar,
         Create Space Independent Publishing Platform (2017)

'Q' and 'A' In A Parallel Universe

Q1   **So, what is the meaning and significance of the equation E=mc²?**

A1   I'll try to answer that question:
About 30 million quarks collided with the same number (except one) of antiquarks in each neighbourhood during that first microsecond of the Big Bang. The collision resulted in the annihilation of all Quarks and Antiquarks, except that one quark that could not find its antiquark. You and I are made up of such surplus quarks that could not be annihilated and hence we arrived in the universe.

That large-scale annihilation of matter/antimatter resulted in a stupendous burst of energy in accordance with the equation $E=mc^2$, and this is what brought about all that radiation. Our freedom as a single quark was quite short-lived; in less than a microsecond, two other quarks joined each of us, and together, as a trio of quarks, we got bigger and became a proton or maybe a neutron, with the former having an 80 percent probability and the latter about 20 percent.

Q2   **Oh, great. So, I got some mass with that "God particle" inside of me? The one they call "Higgs boson"?**

A2   It was the media that called it the "God particle," and the scientists did not mind the publicity. Actually, it was neither God nor particle; it was a boson, and a boson is a force and not a particle. A proton consists of three quarks (two up quarks and one down quark) and of nothing else but these three quarks. The funny thing is that the proton mass is nearly hundred times the total mass of the three

quarks, even though there is nothing else beside the three
quarks in the proton. The three quarks add up to just
about 1 percent of the total mass of the proton.

Q3   **Where does the remaining 99 percent of the mass come
from?**

A3   It's from the strong force that binds the three quarks inside
the proton. Try to pull them apart; try to separate them. You
need an enormous amount of energy to do that. When you
apply the equation $E=mc^2$, you know that there is mass over
there. So, it's a boson and not a particle. Higgs was the
scientist who thought of this first in 1964, and so they named
it the Higgs boson.

Q4   **You're joking! You can't get away with that; you say
that the mass comes from the force. Now, tell me.
Where does the force come from?**

A4   Hmm. I guess there is a 'field' out there in addition to the
gravitational field and the electromagnetic field. Let's call it
the Higgs field. In this Higgs field, trillions of quarks and
antiquarks are arriving and then annihilating each other. In
the end, nothing is left except the energy acquired from all
the collisions, which becomes the force that binds the
quarks that arrive (that is, those quarks that fail to find
their antiquarks and thus do not get annihilated).

Q5   **Such as those inside you and me?**

A5   Exactly. And when these quarks inside you and me
arrived in this aeon of the universe during that first
microsecond after the big bang, all they did was just
progress through the Higgs Field.

Q6   **So, the mass is actually nothing other than a
manifestation of fundamental particles trying to
progress through the Higgs field.**

A6   You are right … I think.

178

Q7   **All that is well and good. But actually, that was not the answer I was looking for w.r.t the significance of the equation E=mc².**

A7   I can only think of one break-away theory to be considered. Einstein warned us about the math. I believe the final computation was something of a dilemma. That the mass of something that actually hits the speed C changes to 1/0, which would create a black hole as far as pure math goes.

Yes, Einstein warned us about the math, when he said that:
"Its not good to introduce the concept of the mass M=m/(1 – v*v/c*c)^0.5 of a moving body for which no clear definition can be given, and it is better to introduce no other mass concept then the rest mass m0."

Note that even as v gets as much as 85 percent of c, the mass M barely doubles the rest mass, and even at 99 percent of c, it is still about 7 times the rest mass. Yes, the final computation was something of a dilemma, and it is better to consider the expression for the momentum and energy of a body in motion, and that as v gets almost equal to c, the square root expression approaches zero and it is the momentum therefore that goes towards infinity.

Q8   **Great, still that is not the answer I was looking for with regards to the significance of the equation 'E=mc²'**

A8   Hmmm……I'll try once more:

The equation led to the discovery of fission, that led to the race for supremacy for developing an atomic bomb, that led to the Manhattan Project, to the bombing of Hiroshima

179

and Nagasaki, and so on, finally leading to the current
situation where we have as many as about twenty
thousand nuclear warheads on the planet Earth, and not
all of them are in safe hands.

And I do believe that the equation $E=mc^2$ should be used
for the development of the world and not its destruction.

- THE END -

AUTHOR'S NOTE AND ACKNOWLEDGEMENTS

"We shall disappear if we cannot adapt to an environment that now contains spaceships, computers and thermonuclear weapons." - Arthur C Clarke

We, human beings are privileged to be among the many intelligent civilizations in the cosmos. But there is nothing special or unique about any of these intelligent civilizations, including human beings. All forms of life including Intelligent Life are products of 'Information' in the 'Intelligent Field.'   But the scope of work of the Intelligent Field is limited to providing life and consciousness only, which in turn is commensurate with the nature of available biochemistry, and there is nothing divine about the 'IF'. This can be gauged from the fact that for the greatest part, life gets rapidly annihilated or cast as prey before other life, to feed it. The 'IF' will not come to the rescue of the human civilization if it is in trouble and facing possible extinction.

Here, I must admit, that the writer of these kind of books that try to predict the 'extinction' of the human race in a certain period of time, is faced with a problem. For, if the human race survives that period of time, he or she is obviously proved wrong, and if the human civilization goes extinct, then there is no one left to say that he or she was right. So, I add the five words "If good sense remains elusive" before making the prediction, give my two cents view on what 'good sense' is, and then hope for the best. The trouble is that the Intelligent Field is unaware of what is 'good' or 'bad'. It will only 'process' the information that comes to it, and the 'effect' will always be a measure of the 'cause'.
So, it boils down to the realisation that for the continued existence of human beings on the planet Earth, the 'bad' information must be 'reduced' or 'deleted all together', and the 'IF' must be flooded, as

181

far as possible, with `good' information only. By 'deleted' it is of course implied that it (the information) should not be allowed to become a 'cause' for any adverse 'effect'. In short it should lose relevance.

As in mathematics, we first differentiate to understand the problem and then integrate to find the solution.

Hence the job in hand - in the writing of this book - was to first make available all the 'information' and then differentiate the 'good' parts that should be retained, from the 'bad' parts that should be deleted.

I do realise that the 'extinction clock' takes into account a variety of factors such as human-caused climate change, disruptive technologies, etc., apart from nuclear dangers. In my book, however, I am somewhat more focused on the nuclear landscape. In my view, a Nuclear Armageddon has the potential to bring about our end in a very short time; perhaps in a matter of days, whereas other factors may take much longer and act far more lingeringly over a period of decades. Hopefully good sense will prevail well in time to save humanity.

So, in the first chapter 'Information in the Field' - which actually should have been 'Information in the Nuclear Field' - the task at hand was to provide all information - good or bad - that has brought us to our current state. A state where we, human beings are required to adapt to an environment that now contains thermonuclear weapons.

It is here that I begin my Acknowledgements.

Yes, I acknowledge with deep thanks all the people - scientists, writers, authors of books, journals, articles, blogs, etc., for transmitting all that information while I was sitting comfortably in my study room. I hope I am not missing any names.

I start with my thanks to Albert Einstein, for giving us the equation E = mc2, which changed the course of history; for his letter to President Roosevelt that resulted in the setting up of the Manhattan Project. Thanks to Ronald W. Clarke for the book 'Einstein: The Life and Times' and to Harry Woolf editor of 'Some Strangeness in the Proportion.' Thanks to Lise Meitner for the discovery of Fission, and to Ruth Lewin Sime, author of 'Lise Meitner: A Life in Physics.' Thanks to Winston Churchill for his many quotations, and to Graham Farmelo for the book 'Churchill's Bombs.' Thanks to Cynthia C. Kelley, editor of the book 'The Manhattan Project'. Passages were selected from the sections 'Dropping the Bombs' and 'Living with the Bomb – A Cold War Warning' from here. Thanks to Joseph Rotblat for his enormous role in spearheading the Pugwash conferences, and his significant contribution towards peace in the world during the cold war. Thanks to Andrew Brown, author of the book 'Keeper of the Nuclear Conscience', passages were selected from the section 'Years of Eclipse' and 'The Latent Progress.' Thanks to James Martin, author of 'The Meaning of the 21st Century.' Thanks to Strobe Talbot, author of the article 'Engaging India: Diplomacy, Democracy and the Bomb' for the extracts relating to the 'Kargil War of 1999.'

Thanks to Noam Chomsky, author of 'What We Say Goes' for extracts relating to 'American Interferences'.

Many thanks to the 'Bulletin of Atomic Scientists' for including my name in their mailing list and regularly sending their newsletters along with many other important articles written by prominent scientists and writers. Thanks to Janice Sinclaire, their Communications Director, for corresponding with me on the subject via emails, answering some of my questions and explaining that 'the clock is not a predictor of nuclear attack, it is a metaphor for the end of humanity, and the time is set by taking into account a variety of factors, including human-caused climate change and disruptive technologies. She also provided several links to background on the clock and how it works. The articles referred in the links were immensely useful in creating a better understanding of the subject and of the significant role played by the 'Bulletin Group' towards peace in the world. For the past seventy years - as revealed in the articles - the doomsday clock has served as a clarion call to all of us - scientists, policy makers, artists, and ordinary citizens, to get engaged and help build a safer and healthier planet. The time for world leaders to address the looming nuclear danger and continuing march of climate change is long past. The time for citizens of the world to demand such action is now. Thanks to Max Tegmark for one of these articles, viz 'A posthumous honour for the man who saved the world.'

In the same way, many thanks to the Pugwash group for including my name in the mailing list and sending regularly their newsletters and eye-opening articles by prominent scientists and writers including some by the President of the Group. Extracts from some of these articles, as well as from the Pugwash website have been used in the manuscript.

My deep thanks are due to Prof. M.S. Swaminathan, Ex-President of the Pugwash group for his support and help. I take pride in the fact that he has read all of my books. He provided the foreword for my second book 'Intelligent Field' and also provided a short but invaluable few lines in praise of 'Bright Light In The Sky.'

I also thank Prof. Charles Townes, famous scientist and inventor of the laser. He along with Prof. M. S. Swaminathan, were among the speakers at the 2003 Symposium on 'Science and Beyond' held in Bangalore. Some extracts from their talks in the seminar have also been included in the manuscript of Chapter 1.

Thanks to V. R. Raghavan for his review of the book 'India's Sentinel', which is on Air Commodre Jasjit Singh's select writing. Extracts have been taken from this in the manuscript. Many thanks to Mike Adams, for his blog on investmentwatchblog.com. This is an eye-opening blog that gives a fairly good indication of the current mind-set of the leaders of the three great nations - US,

Russia and China. Extracts from this blog have been used in a big way to keep the story crisp and engaging. The blog relates to the nuclear test carried out by the US in California in November 2015. This test caused the 'Bright Light in the Sky'.

In chapter three, in order to drive home the points made by me pertaining to the intelligent field and its linkage with the information in the field, I responded to some quotations from two books dealing with the subject of information theory – 'Information and the Nature of Reality', edited by Paul Davies and Niels Henrik Gregersen and 'The New Quantum Age', by Andrew Whitaker. My thanks are due to Paul Davies and Niels Henrik Gregersen, as well as to the authors of the various chapters of the book - Terrence W. Deacon, Seth Lloyd, Jesper Hoffmeyer, Keith Ward, Philip Clayton, Henry Stapp, and Michael Welker, not forgetting the scientist Lee Smolin for his quote in the book 'The New Quantum Age'. Many thanks to Prof. Roger Penrose for the quote from his book 'The Emperor's New Mind'.

For chapter five titled 'Switched On - Arguments for and against a Simulated Universe', I thank the scientist Mario Livio, for his blog 'Can black holes tell us something about digital computers' on Huffington Post, in response to which there was a long conversation between me – who initiated the discussions – and two others 'Charlie Fox Trot' and 'Diogenes of Alaska'. These are pseudo names; I do not know their real names. Nevertheless, I thank them for their views and comments. The chapter is predominantly made up of extracts from this conversation.

Thanks to Sumit Chowdhury, Sudhakar Hannda and Ashok Dwarakanath for their contribution in the development of the book, to my lovely artist wife for her unstinted support. Her exhibition of 26 abstract paintings on 'Intelligent Field' held at the gallery 'Time and Space' in November 2017, was a big success. I expect her to hold a similar one on 'Bright Light In The Sky'.

I also thank Shri A. K. Chandrashekhar, Prof. Ashok Kumar Jain, Dr. Clifton Meador, and Mr. Shoumen Datta for their kind words and their continued support in the development of my books. The imaginative cover design - front and back pages - was the result of a collective effort. Many interesting alternatives were considered before finalising. Thanks to Sudhakar Hannda, Riddhi Mishra (Main contributor), Sumit Chowdhury, my wife Bharati Sagar, not forgetting Mansi Engineer and others from the publisher's team. Thanks to my sons Kamal Sagar and Nikhil Sagar, daughter in law Shibanee Sagar, and M. K. Meador for their help and support. Thanks to Sudhakar Hannda for introducing me to the publisher 'AND ALL', for complete coordination with the publisher at every stage including editing, layout, and cover design, etc. The process of coordination will continue post publishing in all promotional activities including book launches, etc.

I thank the dedicated team of 'AND ALL' for a very professional job of editing, layout and design.

Lastly a few words on my thought process pertaining to the conspiracy theory relating to the 9/11 attacks on the twin towers of the World Trade Center. It is difficult for anyone to provide a satisfactory explanation on what exactly happened; about as difficult to explain as 'what happened at the Big Bang'. The relevant 'information in the field' is privy to may be just a few persons and it is unlikely that the chapter will be reopened for further investigations. Nevertheless, my thanks to the two experts who provided their opinions on the subject, as well as to my friend Salim Sheikh for his comment, which has been extracted in the relevant chapter. Whatever 'UNKNOWNS' in the theory may be, what is definitely 'KNOWN' is that a few human beings killed a large number of human beings.

It is improper to blame a nation or a few nations for the conflicts in the world. A nation is just a geographical area; it is the leaders of some nations who have contaminated the 'Intelligent Field' who must be held accountable.They should either be 'Educated' or

186

'Replaced' by intelligent, knowledgeable and compassionate leaders to make good the contamination.

Last but not the least, I am thankful to the readers for taking the time to read this book. I request and urge them to get involved in whatever way they can to help in the continuation of the 'extraordinary intelligent life' on this wonderful planet Earth.

———

AUTHOR`S NOTE ON THE SECOND EDITION

`` Updated the `Information In The Field` upto November 2019.
Added few paragraphs in chapter five under the sub heading ` TIME
IS RUNNING OUT .. IT IS TIME TO ACT`. Added three reviews on
`Bright Light In The Sky` plus two reviews on my new book `Switched
On`.

At this stage it is pertinent to write a few lines about `Switched On`.

`Switched On` is a Play in two acts about a seminar held in a parallel
universe, where the Participants (mostly scientists and philosophers)
discuss the world situation which is substantially stage-managed by
the Deep States of America and the world. The 9/11 conspiracy
theory is analysed and discussed extensively in the play, and the
participants in the play reach a consensus view-point that the
Evidence .. not of what happened on 9/11, but of what `did not
happen` as alleged to have happened .. lies in the statement
``Newton`s laws cannot be violated``. In other words, given the
inputs relating to the Structural framework (with dimensions) of the
WTC Towers and the structure of the plane (with dimensions)
alleged to have struck the Tower, it is literally impossible for the
planes to have pierced through and completely entered inside the
building without violating Newton`s third law.

That of course was what happened in a parallel universe. What
happens in this universe remains to be seen.

The two books `Switched On` and this revised version of `Bright Light
In the Sky` complement each other with similar objective, viz
`Resolution of conflicts and wars`. Like my other books ``Six Words``
and ``Intelligent Field`` these too are an in-depth exploration into
how humans can come together to change the course of history.

The ultimate objective is peace in the world.

www.ingramcontent.com/pod-product-compliance
Lightning Source LLC
Chambersburg PA
CBHW031110250726

48655CB00004B/1652